Episcopal Curriculum for Youth

Called Through Faith
Leader's Guide

Copyright 1997 by Virginia Theological Seminary and Morehouse Publishing

Copyright 1997 by Virginia Theological Seminary and Morehouse Publishing

All rights reserved. No part of this book may be reproduced, stored in a retrieval system, or transmitted in any form or by any means, electronic, mechanical, photocopying, recording, or otherwise, without the written permission of the publisher.

All Scripture quotations are taken from the New Revised Standard Version, unless otherwise noted.

Developed by
Virginia Theological Seminary
Center for the Ministry of Teaching
3737 Seminary Road
Alexandria, VA 22304

Published by
Morehouse Publishing
P.O. Box 1321
Harrisburg, PA 17105

Amelia J. Gearey, Ph.D., Editor-in-Chief

Dorothy S. Linthicum, Managing Editor

George J. Kroupa, III, Associate Editor

Writers for *Called Through Faith*
    The Rev. Carol Gallagher
    The Rev. Claudia Gould
    The Rev. David Ware

Cover Photo: SuperStock

Design and layout by Jan E. Moffatt, Alexandria, VA.

To Order additional Copies
Call or Write:
    Morehouse Publishing
    Harrisburg, PA

    Toll Free: 1-800-877-0012

ISBN: 0-8192-6052-5

Printed in the United States of America

TABLE OF CONTENTS

Page

BACKGROUND FOR LEADERS
Teaching Youth in Episcopal Churches... 1
Understanding Younger Youth... 3
Who Are Leaders?... 6
The Episcopal Curriculum for Youth... 10
Using the Curriculum.. 11
Called Through Faith.. 12

Called Through Faith: SESSION TITLES
Ambrose: Eloquence for Christ.. 15
Columba: Building Community... 19
Thomas à Becket: Choosing God... 23
Joan of Arc: Soldier for Christ.. 27
Thomas Cranmer: Building on a Foundation... 31
Robert Raikes: Teaching the Gospel.. 35
Amy Carmichael: Saving the Poor... 39
Dietrich Bonhoeffer: Facing Evil.. 43
Oscar Romero: Taking a Stand... 47

BACKGROUND FOR LEADERS

TEACHING YOUTH IN EPISCOPAL CHURCHES

The aim of Christian education in Episcopal Church parishes and congregations is to assist every member in living out the covenant made in Holy Baptism (*The Book of Common Prayer,* page 304). Hence, the common ministry of leaders and youth focuses on matters of both faith and practice:

- **Faith** in God who made heaven and earth, in Jesus Christ the Son of God, and in the Holy Spirit who is Lord and giver of life.
- **Practice** of worship and prayer, of repentance and obedience, of loving service to all persons, and of active pursuit of God's justice and peace in the world.

The content of our faith and practice is continually re-examined and corrected as we search Holy Scripture and the preserved tradition of the Church.

In the words of the Baptismal Covenant, we promise to "continue in the apostles' teaching and fellowship, in the breaking of bread, and in the prayers" (*The Book of Common Prayer*, p. 304). Holy Eucharist, the central act of worship for Christians, unites us with Jesus Christ our Lord. Again and again, as we partake of this sacrament, we remember and celebrate the life and ministry of Jesus Christ.

We are called to follow Jesus, the Son of God, who lived among us as teacher, preacher, and healer. Through his powerful example, Christians have come to understand that the act of teaching is fundamental to our faith.

Teaching Is a Ministry

All Christians are teachers. Our daily lives bear witness to what we believe and treasure. Youth and leaders in the church are poised to share a singular experience that goes beyond the facts and activities of the moment. The aim of Christian education is to assist all members of the Church to discern the signs and spirits of the age and to bring sound theological judgment to bear upon what we observe and experience.

The educative task in a parish or mission is a joint effort of clergy, parents, leaders, and others in the congregation. We cannot rely solely on organized classes for the instruction and nurturing of individuals. With the help and support of the whole congregation, by word and example, by prayers and witness, we seek to bring up young people in the Christian faith and way of life.

Guidelines for Youth

The teenage years can be a time of special opportunities for encountering the invigorating challenge and abiding hope of the Christian gospel. Adolescents are continuing their journeys as full members of the Church, capable of taking part in all aspects of its governance and mission in the world. Within the Baptismal Covenant, this means worshiping and learning in the Christian community, resisting evil, proclaiming the Good News of God in Christ, seeking to serve Christ in all persons, striving for justice and peace, and respecting the dignity of all human beings.

The scriptural teachings of our faith should be affirmed in programs for adolescents. Faith fosters a personal relationship with God and enriches every human relationship. Youth need the Church's encouragement to think critically and independently as they mature in faith.

The ongoing process of faith formation takes on particular relevance for adolescents who are coming up against questions of personal identity and life choices. That is why churches need to focus on welcoming and including young persons in every possible way.

Gifts of Youth. Adolescence is a time of questioning, debating, and searching. The faith of young Christians thrives when they are enabled to use their own talents and abilities in pursuit of the Church's mission, working with their peers alongside experienced adults.

Among the gifts adolescents bring are spontaneity, ebullience, vision, creative energies, and the ability to challenge existing structures and habits of the institution. As their convictions find focus and voice, earnest young Christians provide windows into God's presence and sometimes offer surprising perspectives for viewing the nature of God and the work of the Holy Spirit.

Counter Culture. An increasingly diverse, secular society tends to foster discrete groups with a variety of life styles. There are ever-changing forms of music, art, dress, language, and behavior. Adolescents are particularly susceptible to the societal influences of media presentations, advertising, and marketing. They manifest and live in what is popularly termed "youth culture."

The Christian faith, at its best, has always been a counter culture with a corrective and saving message for all who seek purpose and meaning in their lives. Christian educators strive to be fully informed about where youth are "coming from" in order to explore with mutual respect the claims of God in Christ.

Christian education can help youth to identify the tugging forces in their world. Many teenagers search for strength to handle difficult issues of theology, family life, relationships with friends, peace and justice, and ethics. The challenge is to find appropriate and respectful ways to interact with the vernacular of young people. If, in our ministry with adolescents, we try too hard to speak the language of youth culture, we run the risk of failing to share plainly the Church's good news.

Distinctiveness. Rapid physical, emotional, and intellectual changes occur during the teenage years. Sexual maturation proceeds rapidly. Social awkwardness and self-consciousness are often apparent. The role and timing of developmental changes may vary greatly among boys and girls throughout adolescence.

The challenge of ministry with youth is to meet the specific needs of youth with varied and appealing programs. Education for adolescents necessarily takes on a different look and style from programs for younger learners. An appropriate balance is necessary between active involvement of youth and lecture and instruction.

Continuity. It is desirable that people who work with youth have a mutually developed sense of purpose. Formal, integrated programs of teaching and learning, using suitable curricular resources, are needed.

At the same time, it is essential to maintain a sense of continuity in Christian education for the entire congregation as one people of God. At all age levels, we have a common need to know who we are as Episcopalians in the worldwide body of Christ.

Flexibility. Episcopal congregations schedule teaching and learning in different ways and at different times. Realistic assessment of the time demands on youth is essential in planning programs for adolescents. It is important to take into account young persons' commitments within their families and the wider community.

The principle of flexibility is particularly appropriate for developing study materials for use in the Church's ministry with adolescents. Especially desirable are themes of study that can be adjusted to varying lengths of time, with modules designed to be arranged in a variety of sequences.

Groupings. Experience in general education suggests a workable approach for grouping adolescents: *Younger Youth* (ages 12-14, Junior High or Middle School grades) and *Older Youth* (ages 15-18, Senior High grades). In congregations where multiple groups are not feasible, a single youth group is best supported by flexible resources, adaptable to a range of developmental levels and interests.

UNDERSTANDING YOUNGER YOUTH

Who are the younger youth we teach? The key to understanding this age group lies in a heart-felt, enduring respect for youth as individuals. Such respect, accompanied by knowledge of the differences among us, shapes all our efforts as teachers.

Look closely at any group of young people, and it is readily apparent that on physical characteristics alone, there is considerable diversity within the group. Reflect further on the impact of different social and ethnic backgrounds, economic circumstances, schooling opportunities, skills and interests, and it becomes quite clear that narrow descriptions do not reflect the dizzying array of social and cultural diversity present among youth of the same chronological age. To teach youth as individuals requires that we first see them as individuals. We can turn to important sources of information:

- **Developmental theory** offers insights for the teaching task. Customarily, educators have looked primarily to such theories for help in understanding the growth and development of children. Younger youth are well past the early stages of development, however, and no single developmental viewpoint appears to be adequate by itself to provide a comprehensive basis for planning instruction.
- **Literature** is another source. Stories of youth enable adults to reconnect with adolescents and to experience, vicariously, radically different life-shaping situations.
- **Experiences** of teachers themselves can contribute much reliable information, including memories of their own journeys as young people.

Taken in combination, these three sources—theory, literature, and experience—contribute to a distinctive multi-dimensional perspective on the lives and learning of young people. This blend of insights will be especially helpful for teachers in church school settings.

Theory—A Source of Information

Developmental theories help us to see the expected, sequential patterns of change from birth through maturity. All theories of development hold that increasing maturity brings a general increase in the complexity of behavior. Children move away from self-centeredness toward more social autonomy. Regardless of whether a theory uses ages or stages, the emphasis is on general expectations. No theory can completely predict the behavior of an individual.

Most of the mainstream theories were formulated without particular regard for the effect of gender. Today, we are living (and teaching) amidst a greater sensitivity to issues of developmental differences between girls and boys. (See Carol Gilligan's book, *In a Different Voice*, for an enlightening discussion on this topic.)

Thinking. We owe much to the Swiss psychologist, Jean Piaget, for underscoring the fact that the ability to think and form ideas changes as one matures and develops. Using cognitive stages, which may be loosely associated with ages, he defined the ways of knowing that move from sensing to concrete knowing to abstract thinking. According to Piaget, younger youth have just begun to use increasingly complex mental operations and are no longer constricted by what they can see. They can think about situations from more than one point of view, handle several ideas at once, and can move back and forth in relation to a particular idea. Around age eleven, the most advanced level of cognitive functioning may be reached. At this point, youth (and presumably, all adults) can imagine possibilities, reason abstractly, and think across time—past, present and future. All individuals move back and forth in these stages when new and unfamiliar concepts are encountered.

A note of caution: Cognitive theories do not specify *what* content students should be thinking about. And, perhaps more critically, Piaget's stages of knowing do not uniformly apply to youth from different social-cultural environments. Many observers feel that variations in life experience can dramatically alter the ages at which various types of cognitive functioning are likely to emerge.

Social context. During the adolescent years, youth increase and consolidate previous developmental gains in the context of an enlarging social group—family, friends, and community. Personal interests dictate much of what they are most likely to do. Parental supervision is giving way to self-supervision and independence.

Erik Erikson's work postulates a view of development that interweaves the powerful impact of social context with ongoing biological maturation. According to Erikson, at each of eight stages in life a major psychosocial crisis must be resolved in order for development to proceed. In Stage V, the teenage years, the dominant developmental crisis revolves around identity versus role-confusion. It is a period of confusion, searching, and experimenting with a variety of roles for future choices. A sense of loyalty for different groups often causes conflict within an individual.

Work by Lawrence Kohlberg, related to moral development, has melded ideas from both social and cognitive theory. With maturation, experience, and expanding strategies for thinking, youth and adults approach and resolve moral dilemmas in more complex ways.

Each of these theorists gives us a broader insight into the complicated interactive processes of development. While none of them specifically addresses the growth of religious thought, their work has underscored recent efforts to depict faith development for children and adults.

Literature—A Source of Understanding

Literature helps to expand our awareness of the wide variety of experiences of adolescents. Whatever the circumstances of our own youth, literature offers a credible opportunity to "walk in someone else's moccasins." Teachers of younger youth will be enriched by reading some of the novels about the struggles of young people.

Contemporary writers such as Madeleine L'Engle, and Cynthia Voigt introduce us to a modern generation of youth with complex issues, fantasies, struggles, and challenges which reflect still another generation's efforts to deal with the universal themes. David Elkind and Michael Warren have written prophetically about the stressful and hurried lives of youth today.

Experience—A Source of Connection

The teen-age years are for most people traumatic. Very few individuals would wish to relive their teen years.

Ask yourself: In seventh grade, who were your friends? Your neighbors? Your favorite teachers? In the eighth grade? Ninth grade? How did you spend your time outside of school? Lastly, how many times have you said to a young person, "When I was your age, I . . . ."

Our own youth—with all the glories and all the miseries—generally becomes a subjective yardstick for measuring the events in the lives of our students. On a rational level, we know that students today have vastly different experiences at school, in the community, and with friends. The textures of their daily environments, both physical and economic, are critically different. Space missions are routine, and viewers literally watch in real-time as wars are televised.

Nevertheless, certain aspects of adolescence remain virtually unchanged across the years. Successes, failures, feelings, doubts, joys, and struggles remain a vital part of students' daily lives. Universal themes are evident in the questions youth ask and the answers they seek: "Who am I? Whose am I? Why am I here? What should I do? Where am I going?" It is essential to acknowledge that these themes exist. They were part of our own youth and now become a powerful link with today's students.

Faith in the Classroom

> Faith is a gift from God.
> We are people of faith.

These two premises underlie all that we say and do in church school classrooms. It is faith that gives church school its unique mission. We do not teach faith. We can surely hope that our work as teachers will nurture faith in the hearts and minds of our students.

Structure of Faith

Teachers can interpret the actions and responses of their students better by knowing that faith is personal, always changing and growing. A widely-discussed model of faith development uses a pyramid framework of ages and stages to illuminate modal characteristics of faith across the life cycle.

According to James Fowler, younger youth are literalists (Stage 3: Synthetic-Conventional Faith), looking primarily beyond the family to other spheres. Faith provides a basis for identity.

In contrast, John Westerhoff uses the image of concentric rings to portray how faith grows and matures within the web of relationships in a faith community. In his model, the faith of adolescents is one of belonging to a faith community (affiliative faith) yet moving beyond to question the faith of our parents (searching faith). The title of Westerhoff's book, *Will Our Children Have Faith?* (1976), still resonates among leaders in Christian education.

Who are Youth?

Volumes have been written on adolescent development. The purpose here is to give leaders of this program some key pointers about the characteristics of younger youth to enable leaders to become effective teachers. This is not an exhaustive list and must be generalized. It is, however, important to be aware of these qualities and needs.

Characteristics of younger youth:

- **They like to have fun.** Fun is not the opposite of learning nor should fun be seen as something to be avoided. On the contrary, people learn best when they are having a good time. When youth are having a good time, they often make a lot of noise. Don't be afraid of a little commotion if most of the group are on task. Encourage your teens to have fun in your class and see how much they will learn.

- **Seek identity.** Younger youth are in an energetic process of seeking who they are, while at the same time, fearing what they may find out. Two key words for the wise leader are: accept and affirm. Accept each person as he or she is; look for qualities in each that you like. Don't try to change them. Affirm the skills, talents, questions, concerns and uniqueness of each person in an intentional way.

- **Like-making choices.** Many adults believe that younger youth should not be allowed to make decisions for themselves because they are too immature. Some people teach without seeking input or options from those they are teaching. Youth make decisions all the time. Our gift to them is to help them to develop their abilities to make good decisions and to treat them as capable human beings.

- **Need to be heard.** One of the best tools you can provide for younger youth are opportunities to speak out and be heard, and to listen to others in the group with respect. It is important to set the example not by what you say but by what you do. Your ability to listen to youth and respond to their ideas and comments will be a model for their own listening skills. Being heard for even a moment can be a powerful experience.

- **Seek approval.** Approval from peers and adults is essential at this age. This need for attention and approval can lead to various expressions of behavior. Some youth will be over-achievers, trying to please by standing out above the rest. Others will seek attention by how they dress, or by the language they use. The skilled leader looks for ways to offer appropriate approval, acceptance, and affirmation while still providing guidelines, boundaries, and expectations.

- **Want to be valued and significant.** How you treat the younger youth in your class is much more important than what you teach. If youth feel important and significant, they are more likely to learn something from the class. It is also crucial to pay attention to how the teens treat each other. The atmosphere of the classroom can enliven or poison the whole experience. Encouraging youth to behave in respectful ways to adults and to one another may be the most important lesson you can teach. Many youth in today's church school classes come from different schools, belong to different clubs and organizations, inside and outside of their schools. Building a successful group that reaches out in hospitality to newcomers and those on the fringes is one of the main goals of working with younger youth. It is also the message of the gospel.

- **More interested in who's there than what is taught.** The friendships that already exist and the friendships that develop are often the motivating factor for attendance and learning. The skilled teacher supports and encourages these relationships while trying to avoid cliques that exclude others. A key word here is inclusiveness.

- **Growing and changing.** Everything about this time in the lives of younger youth calls them to grow in mind, body and spirit. The hunger to grow (often subconscious) is a great ingredient for learning. Youth want to know more about the things that affect their lives. This includes God and knowing Jesus Christ. However, they also change constantly which makes them unpredictable. Accept these deep down longings and ever-changing attitudes as gifts.

- **Looking for a faith of their own.** Younger youth are seeking their own opinions, values, and faith. Their identity comes from becoming their own person. Youth often reject much of their parent's faith. This is an important sign that new values and a stronger faith are being formed. Embrace the searching process and affirm the importance of the ability to question, doubt and think. Your response to their doubts will encourage or discourage their journeys to spiritual knowledge. Their questions will ultimately lead to faith.

WHO ARE LEADERS?

Leaders of youth are more than teachers. To foster effective teaching and learning among its adolescent members, the Church needs adult leaders who are grounded in their own faith and identity as Christians. Effective leaders are excited about growing and learning and enjoy working with youth in a team relationship. They have high energy, genuine enthusiasm, and a passionate interest in youth.

Because church leaders are expected to have a unique relationship with youth, the teacher/student relationship does not work well on Sunday morning with younger youth. Teens have been in that role all week and want something different. While it is important to share knowledge, it is more important to develop a group that can share their faith. Here are some characteristics commonly found in effective youth leaders.

- **Rooted in their faith and committed to Jesus Christ.** Who leaders are speaks loudly to teens. This doesn't mean that leaders have to be biblical scholars or perfect Christians. It also doesn't mean they no longer have any doubts or are at the end of their own spiritual journey. Good leaders have a strong relationship with God and are comfortable with their faith.

- **Is willing to be a part of a team.** Helping a young person to grow in the knowledge and love of the Lord is an overwhelming task. It is essential for leaders to understand that they do not have sole responsibility for this task. Wise leaders know that they are not only part of a teaching team but also part of a network of people in the church who care about and support young people.

- **Is fun and enjoys being with young people.** A key phrase to help leaders is "relax and enjoy." Effective leaders know how to have fun and to share joy with young people without giving up expectations of them. Leaders must find their own balance of fun and seriousness. Affirming joy and excitement with the group, however, is essential for the leaders' full participation.

- **More concerned about people than facts.** The ECY provides an excellent base of information to learn more about God, scripture and the Church. The sessions incorporate this learning with the issues that effect young people's lives. Effective leaders are aware of issues that are unique to their groups and look for ways to include these ideas in their presentations. When leaders give priority to what youth are thinking and feeling, the content follows.

- **Has a long-term commitment to the group.** Good leaders are committed and consistent. There will be ups and downs, and successes and failures. Some weeks the youth may be impossible to reach, but the steadfastness of faith and commitment to the class will make a real difference in the long run. Focus on the overall success of the program and not on any one moment, hour, or week.

Building the Team

The *Episcopal Curriculum for Youth* is designed to be used with a team approach. Having more than one leader allows young people to have a variety of models of Christian faith. Young people relate to different adults in unique ways. This range of relationships and friendships is important. Also, the team approach allows for mutual support of the adult leaders.

Sometimes an adult leader will see an issue raised by a youth as a challenge to authority. Another leader may have a different perception of what is causing the conflict and be able to step in to maintain the relationships. It is also essential for reasons of safety and protection to have teams of adults working together at all times. Finally, each person has different gifts. When each of the gifts are given together they far exceed the gifts of one individual.

The best way to function well as a team is to spend a block of time together before the year begins. It is ideal to have eight to ten hours for this purpose. The team may decide to meet several times or go on retreat somewhere for this purpose. The team should decide which setting works best for them.

Suggested activities to help the team plan their strategies are outlined below:

- **Begin with social time** together, including sharing basic facts about each other.

- **Share faith stories.** A simple way to do this is to ask people to make a chart from birth to the present showing the highlights and low moments of their faith journey. Allow time for everyone to finish before sharing so each person can listen to each presentation.

- **Make a list of each person's gifts** and identify the gifts, talents or interests that he or she would like to contribute to the class.

- **Working Together.** Discuss how the team will work together including roles, tasks, and schedules. Be sure to include in your discussion how young people will be used as leaders in this program (see section on youth as leaders).

- **Review the curriculum materials** together and discuss the best ways for the team to use them.

- **Planning.** Draw up a plan for the year with clear responsibilities for each team member.

- **Leaders need information and training.** Any effective leadership program begins with the sharing of information and the training of skills. This is no less true for Christian leaders. The ECY offers materials to provide a strong base of information about scripture, theology and the Church.

- **Teamwork does not mean just rotating Sundays.** A true team requires blending-together time, talents, skills and gifts. The team should discuss and clarify the ways they will work together before beginning. The team should feel both energized and excited as they initiate this venture.

Youth as Leaders

Young people are able to assume responsibility for their own learning. As leaders they help to plan and to carry out programs. It is imperative that adolescents develop a sense of real ownership and personal investment in the Church's life and mission. They need assurance that their decisions and contributions are respected and valued.

A basic premise of this curriculum is to not only teach students but also raise up Christian leaders. Many young people have outstanding leadership qualities. These qualities can be used to develop an exciting program of learning and growth. Often adult leaders overlook or ignore the leadership capabilities of younger youth who have so much to offer. Do not make this mistake. The following list will help you to recognize, build, and utilize the youth leadership of the group.

- **Sharing Information.** In order for youth to participate effectively in planning for and leading a group, they must have the basic information available to leaders and be able to make choices of their own.

- **Training usually involves practice.** Allowing the teens to try out new ideas, theologies and skills in a safe environment is a great way to train them for leadership roles. Giving them opportunities to lead the group is a way to practice the gifts and talents that God has given them.

- **Young people are not "blank slates."** The youth in the group come with a richness of ideas, thoughts, opinions, and experiences. They are not empty, inexperienced human beings just waiting to receive facts and gems of wisdom. They have as much to teach as they have to learn. Often they are so used to being treated like "blank slates" that they are reluctant to share all that they have to offer. When they trust that their experiences and opinions are valued, a whole new world of information, learning and sharing will open up. Encourage this process, and be patient if it takes some time for it to develop.

- **People deserve input into decisions that affect their lives.** Youth in your program deserve to have input into their learning process. Often adult leaders plan the sessions with little or no involvement from those they are trying to reach. This often leads to apathetic learning. Also, the adults miss the benefit of the wisdom and understanding of the youth about their needs, desires and insights. Although the process will be different in each situation, be intentional about learning from the youth both before beginning and then during the sessions.

- **Young people should be responsible for their own learning.** One way to value the participants in the group is to allow them to take responsibility for their learning. This means agreeing ahead of time what will be learned and how the learning will be carried out. A contract or covenant should be established with the group, and the adult leader should hold people accountable to what they have agreed. It will take time to develop the trust for this to happen, but the benefit is enormous.

- **Leadership skills apply to all facets of life.** If adult leaders are successful at lifting up youth leaders, the skills developed will affect other areas of the youth's lives. Youth group members will find themselves involved in leadership roles in their schools, families, churches and other organizations. They will have discovered tools that will last them the rest of their lives. These skills along with their Christian faith will make an impact on all with whom they come in contact.

- **Forming a youth leadership team.** Although a youth leadership team will have many variations depending on each situation, it is recommended that one is formed. This may be as simple as gathering a few young people ahead of time to review the materials and make suggestions on how best to use this curriculum. A team of youth that meet with the adult team regularly and share in planning for the sessions can be developed. Certain sessions or projects could be given to a small group of youth to let them "run with it." It is important that the adult leaders build in some time to plan the role of young people as leaders of this curriculum.

Developmental Resources
Ames, Louise Bates, Ilg, Frances L., & Stanley M. Baker. *Your ten to fourteen-year-old.* New York: Delacorte Press, 1988.
Dillard, Annie. *An American childhood.* New York: Harper & Row, 1987.
Elkind, David. *All grown up and no place to go.* Reading: Addison-Wesley, 1981.
Erikson, Erik H. *Identity, Youth and Crisis.* New York: W. W. Norton, 1968.
Gilligan, Carol. *In a different voice.* Cambridge: Harvard University Press, 1982.
Kozol, Jonathan. *Death at an early age.* New York: Plume/Dutton, 1985.
Kuhmerker, Lisa with Uwe Gielen & Richard L. Hayes. *The Kohlberg legacy for the helping professions.* Birmingham: R.E.P., 1991.
Singer, Dorothy G. & Tracey A. Revenson. *A Piaget primer: How a child thinks.* New York: Plume/New American Library, 1978.
Stevens, Richard. *Erik Erikson: An introduction.* New York: St. Martin's Press, 1983.

Resources on Faith
Aleshire, Daniel O. *Faithcare.* Philadelphia: Westminster Press, 1988.
Fowler, James W. *Stages of faith.* New York: Harper & Row, 1981.
Hyde, Kenneth E. *Religion in childhood and adolescence.* Birmingham: Religious Education Press, 1990.
Stokes, Kenneth. *Faith is a verb.* Mystic: Twenty-Third Publications, 1989.
Westerhoff, John H., III. *Will our children have faith?* New York: Seabury Press, 1976.

Episcopal Resources
The Book of Common Prayer. New York: The Church Hymnal Corporation, 1979.
The Book of Occasional Services. (2nd. ed.) New York: The Church Hymnal Corporation, 1988.
Booty, John E. *What makes us Episcopalians?* Wilton: Morehouse-Barlow, 1982.
Holmes, Urban T., III. *What is Anglicanism?* Wilton: Morehouse-Barlow, 1982.
The Hymnal 1982. New York: The Church Hymnal Corporation, 1985.
Lesser feasts and fasts. (1991 ed.) New York: The Church Hymnal Corporation, 1991.
Molrine, Charlotte N. & Ronald C. Molrine. *Encountering Christ in the Episcopal Church.* Harrisburg: Morehouse Publishing, 1992.
Sydnor, William. *More than words.* San Francisco: Harper & Row, 1990.

Wall, John S. *A new dictionary for Episcopalians.* San Francisco: Harper & Row, 1985.
Westerhoff, John H. *A people called Episcopalians.* Atlanta: St Bartholomew's Episcopal Church, 1993.
When in our music God is glorified.(disks or cassettes) New York: The Church Hymnal Corporation, undated.
Wolf, Barbara. *Journey in faith: An inquirer's program.* (rev. ed.) Minneapolis: Seabury Press, 1982.
Zinser, Henry A. *Continue thine forever.* (2nd ed.) Wilton: Morehouse-Barlow, 1985.

THE EPISCOPAL CURRICULUM FOR YOUTH

The curriculum uses a cumulative framework of twelve modules to be used over a period of years. Designed for younger youth who may be in middle school or junior high, it provides choices for leaders and youth to compose their own unique sequence of lessons. Three of the modules focus on Old Testament (Hebrew Scriptures), three on the New Testament, and three on Contemporary Times. Within each stream are the archetypes of **Call, Covenant,** and **Community.** In addition three modules are on the basics of *Sacraments, The Episcopal Church Year,* and *Spiritual Life.*

	Old Testament	New Testament	Contemporary Times	Basics	
CALL "Who me?" How individuals respond to faith's call offers a treasury of examples of human emotions and conflicts	Called by God (available now)	Called by Jesus (available 1998)	Called through Faith (available now)	Sacraments of the Church (available now)	A look at the meaning and significance of the church sacraments
COVENANT The personal stories of those who led in following the promise of God—and modern questions concerning the covenants	Covenant Ancestors (available now)	New Covenant Disciples (available now)	People of the Promise (available 1998)	The Episcopal Church Year (available now)	Examination of the church seasons and the sights and sounds of church
COMMUNITY By examining the trials and tribulations of people in the faith community, we discover both "Who and Whose we are?"	Community Leaders (available 1998)	Christians Build Community (available now)	Witnesses in the World (available now)	Spiritual Life (available 1998)	From ways of praying to the ethics of the church—a look at the threads that form our personal experiences
	From Amos to Maccabes, a look at Old Testament figures	A focus on people and events from the time of Jesus	Examinations of contemporary and historical figures like C.S. Lewis and Becket	Examinations of church traditions and practices	

A Tool for Teachers

The aim of the *Episcopal Curriculum for Youth* (ECY) is to sustain and strengthen the ministry of teaching in the Episcopal Church. The curriculum's focus on classroom-based efforts does not deny the importance of youth groups, confirmation classes, retreats or other patterns of Christian education in a local congregation. It does reflect an intentional decision to affirm the act of teaching and spotlight the respective roles of teachers and learners.

The curriculum is a tool for teachers. It serves as a resource to help teachers formulate answers to three pivotal questions:

- **What do I teach?** The curriculum offers a series of modules on twelve different topics. Leaders using the materials are expected to pursue actively an adult-level understanding of the content of the session outlines, taking seriously their own roles as learners.

- **Whom do I teach?** Leaders are challenged anew to adapt to both the developmental characteristics of the group as well as the particular interests of each individual. The ECY addresses issues of developmental differences from two important perspectives. Content is developmentally appropriate, using Scripture as a basis for exploring issues with younger youth. Within each session provisions are made in activity suggestions for varying degrees of skill and learning styles among students.

- **How do I teach?** The curriculum was written for leaders by clergy and laity who work with youth. Options and guidelines are included to help leaders make adjustments to fit local circumstances. Embedded in the kaleidoscope of optional activity suggestions given for every session are practical comments and specific tips for guiding the process of learning.

It is hoped that leaders who use the ECY will be nurtured, inspired, and enriched personally as they prepare to teach and learn and as they reflect on their efforts.

Teachers will find that the session outlines in this guide provide support and structure for the inexperienced and both challenge and flexibility for the more confident. It is highly recommended that every leader have ready access to a Bible (NRSV), *The Book of Common Prayer*, and *The Hymnal 1982*. Each session includes the following:

- **Objective** statement, to state the concepts along with objectives.
- **Background for Leaders** and **Personal Views**, to provide factual background and personal inspiration.
- **Tips on the Topic,** to offer useful information about working with this age group.
- **Weavings,** to prompt thinking about how this session fits into the year, vocabulary, and current events.
- **Look For,** to provide thoughts on follow-through of the session.

USING THE CURRICULUM

Planning Class Sessions

Planning sets the stage for teaching and learning. In preparation for meeting with students, teachers need to *select* a set of activities, and then put these activities into an *order* for each class meeting. The session outlines of the *Episcopal Curriculum for Youth* offer three sets of activity categories that can be used to compose a class session. These are:

Teacher Supports—six sections directed at helping teachers prepare.

Essential Activities—Coming Together, Engaging, and Going Forth are the three core experiences for each session.

Optional Activities—a variety of different suggestions of activities, which teachers may choose to do in a given session. *No teacher or class is expected to use every optional activity in any session outline. The stress is on choice.*

The session categories function as the building blocks for planning. There is no single, "right" way to plan a class session. Teachers can construct an activity/time schedule for each class session that fits the time available, builds on their own skills, and meets the needs and interests of youth.

Teachers facilitate classroom activities through interactive planning with youth. Teens will be able to exercise leadership roles in choosing and implementing what they wish to explore. Students' interests will strongly affect the direction of theme exploration and conversation.

Teachers understand their students. Students deserve attention, affirming experiences, and reasonable challenges. To nurture and guide the faith journey of another person demands a personal relationship. Bonds of trust, respect, and affection grow where caring and understanding prevail.

Teachers are interpreters. Students can expect honest answers to their questions—including the response, "I don't know." In classroom situations, what students talk about, question, explore, and wonder about reflects their teachers' ability to mediate and interpret faith and heritage. Often the simplest of questions can evoke profound discussion.

Youth can be intensely interested in wrestling with "real-world" ethical issues. As teachers and students engage in conversations of faith, they are sharing feelings and values, as well as words and facts. In a very real sense, teachers expose their beliefs when they engage in conversation with youth.

The Learning Environment

The setting where the group meets is crucial to the success of the program. In short, the less like a classroom it is, the more you will be able to facilitate learning, sharing, and growth. Pay attention to the environment you are providing, as this will make a great impact on the learning process.

Consider three possibilities to create the desired environment.

- **The youth room.** One good alternative is a room at the church designated for young people and arranged with comfortable chairs, couches, etc. This provides a comfortable and inviting atmosphere.

- **Meeting in a home.** Holding meetings at someone's home who lives nearby the church can be a great asset. This provides a casual, comfortable setting that usually enhances the process. This may provide some logistical problems for younger youth but it is well worth investigating. Also, people may be more open to making their homes available if it is done on a rotating basis. Don't rule out this possibility without carefully considering it.

- **Gathering in a restaurant.** A restaurant can provide a wonderful opportunity for a meal, fellowship, and learning. Often young people who wouldn't come to the church will feel comfortable in this setting. Of course, this will raise some financial considerations, but these are not insurmountable. You could also consider meeting at a restaurant on an occasional basis as a way of promoting outreach and for celebration.

A Final Word

Remember that this is a process of helping young people grow in their knowledge and love of the Lord. There will be ups and downs, successes and failures, joys and frustrations. Often you will never know the impact you have made on a young person's life. So much happens intellectually, emotionally, and spiritually at this time in their lives that they themselves are not aware of the people who have had a direct impact. Share the love of Christ with your young people. Remember that God has called us not to be successful but to be faithful. Thanks be to God.

CALLED THROUGH FAITH

The content of this module focuses on noted individuals in the Church and Call. Titled *Called Through Faith*, each session examines relationships with God and others. Each person's relationship with God is encountered, challenged, and nurtured by their experiences with God. Youth today are also seeking relationships with God, but often encounter doubts and questions. Seeing themselves as Christians in relationships with God in Jesus Christ as they live out the promises of the Baptismal Covenant, is the hoped for outcome of this course of study.

The *Episcopal Curriculum for Youth* provides materials for both leaders and youth.

For Teachers
■ **Leader's Guide** (this volume)
Contains 9 sessions of material. The sessions are:
- *Ambrose: Eloquence for Christ*
- *Columba: Building Community*
- *Thomas à Becket: Choosing God*
- *Joan of Arc: Soldier for Christ*
- *Thomas Cranmer: Building on a Foundation*
- *Robert Raikes: Teaching the Gospel*
- *Amy Carmichael: Saving the Poor*
- *Dietrich Bonhoeffer: Facing Evil*
- *Oscar Romero: Taking a Stand*

■ **Poster Pack**
Offers 6 large sheets of color posters or black-and-white resource posters. Intended for use as a classroom resource.

The Guide and Packet are undated and can be reused. We recommend that congregations have one Leader's Guide for each teacher along with one Poster Pack for each group of youth.

For Students
■ **Session Leaflets** (student leaflets—one for each session)
In attractive, colorful format, each leaflet includes:
Scripture
Commentary and prayer by youth
Illustrations
Voices: thoughts from various authors, politicians, theologians, and others on the session topic
Prayers and words to remember
Bible reflections to read during the week

■ **Bibles and Prayerbooks**
Special editions of the Holy Bible and *The Book of Common Prayer* have been created for the *Episcopal Curriculum for Youth*. It is recommended that each youth have their own copy of these important books of our faith.

■ **Additional Gear**
Backpacks, patches, bookmarks, and bookplates are also available to give youth a sense of belonging and common purpose.

Teaching Resources
Bowman, Locke E., Jr. *Teaching for Christian hearts, souls, and minds.* San Francisco: Harper & Row, 1990.
Farnham, Suzanne G., et. al. *Listening Hearts: Discerning Call in Community.* Harrisburg: Morehouse, 1991.
Little, Sara. *To set one's heart: Belief and teaching in the Church.* Atlanta: John Knox Press, 1983.
Harris, Maria. *Teaching and religious imagination.* San Francisco: Harper & Row, 1987.
Kujawa, Sheryl A. and Sibley, Lois. *Resource Book for Ministry with Youth and Young Adults in the Episcopal Church.* New York: Episcopal Church Center, 1995.

Music Resources
Gather, Volume 1 and Volume 2. GIA Publications, Inc. 7404 South Mason Avenue, Chicago, Illinois 60638, 1994.

Baptist Hymnal. Nashville: Convention Press, 1975.
Glory and Praise, Vol. 2. Phoenix: North American Liturgy Resources, 1982.
Glory and Praise, Vol. 3. Phoenix: North American Liturgy Resources, 1982.
Lift Every Voice and Sing II. New York: The Church Hymnal Corporation, 1993.
Songs for Celebration, Church Hymnal Series IV, New York, The Church Hymnal Corporation, 1980.

Ambrose: Eloquence for Christ
Called through Faith

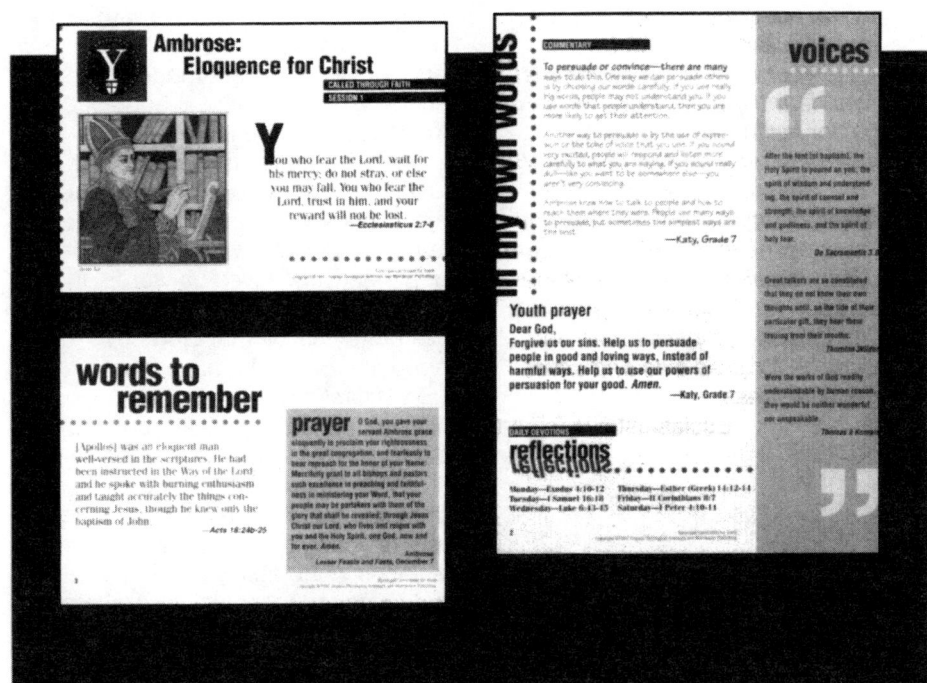

Objective

This session focuses on Bishop Ambrose, a mediator for the Church. Youth will be able to name ways that words can be effective in persuading others to be calm and to change. They will look for ways to use words to make an argument for their views.

Background for Leaders

The Commentary provides information about Ambrose and his influence on the people of Milan. Key people are Ambrose and Augustine; the key place is Milan, Italy. For spiritual preparation, think about how God has helped you overcome feelings of inadequacy.

Commentary

Ambrose is remembered by the Church for his eloquence and calmness in the face of adversity. He was born in the fourth century into a Christian household, although he was never baptized as a child. His family was influential, and his father was governor of Gaul. Before he was elected bishop, Ambrose himself became the governor in Upper Italy.

As governor, he was asked to go to Milan in 373 to mediate the election of the Bishop of Milan. The difficult election pitted Arian and Orthodox Christians against one another. The power of Milan in Church politics elevated the tension of this election.

When faced with the prospect of a divided Church, the people elected Ambrose as bishop, although he was not even a candidate, nor had he been baptized. Ambrose was hastily baptized and ordained bishop on December 7, 373.

Ambrose at first did not think himself adequate to the task of being bishop and protested the people's choice. However, through his God-given gifts of eloquence and mediation, Ambrose rose to the occasion. To the good people of Milan, he wrote:

"Lord Jesus Christ, you are, for me medicine when I am sick; you are my strength when I need help; you are life itself when I fear death...."

Ambrose was able despite the tension of his times to hold the church together by preaching, mediation, clear and practical teaching, and using his gifts for music. He was given the strength and ability to challenge sinful emperors and to make God's love plain to the people in his community. He also was instrumental in the conversion of Augustine, who became one of the most important theologians in Western Christianity.

Ambrose is the model of one who made the gospel simple and approachable, profoundly changing the hearts of many. In his simplicity, he changed the Church and the world.

For further study: Read about Ambrose in *Lesser Feasts and Fasts*, December 7.

SESSION LEAFLET

■ **Art**—*Ambrose*, by Bobbi Tull

■ **Key Verse**—*You who fear the Lord, wait for his mercy; do not stray, or else you may fall. You who fear the Lord, trust in him, and your reward will not be lost.*
—Ecclesiasticus 2:7-8

■ **Youth Commentary and Prayer**

■ **Voices**—De Sacramentis 3.8, Thornton Wilder, Thomas à Kempis

■ **Daily Reflections**

■ **Words to Remember**

■ **Prayer**—Ambrose, *Lesser Feasts and Fasts*, December 7

Episcopal Curriculum for Youth—Called Through Faith
Copyright © 1997 Virginia Theological Seminary and Morehouse Publishing

LECTOR'S TEXT

You who fear the Lord, wait for his mercy; do not stray, or else you may fall. You who fear the Lord, trust in him, and your reward will not be lost. You who fear the Lord, hope for good things, for lasting joy and mercy. Consider the generations of old and see: has anyone trusted in the Lord and been disappointed? Or has anyone persevered in the fear of the Lord and been forsaken? Or has anyone called upon him and been neglected? For the Lord is compassionate and merciful; he forgives sins and saves in time of distress.

Ecclesiasticus 2:7-11

TIPS ON THE TOPIC

- Youth may be uncomfortable admitting they don't know the meaning of words often used in church. Be sure this is a positive experience.
- Public speaking is intimidating for many youth. Let them know that eloquence is not a prerequisite for getting along with others or resolving conflicts.
- **Discussion Starter:** Do you ever feel "lost" at church because you don't understand what people are saying? Describe the situation and your feelings.

Personal Views

A common concern for many of us when working with youth is a sense of inadequacy. Public speaking, particularly in times of crisis, heightens our feelings of inadequacy. In Ambrose, we find a good man, doing his best to keep the peace when all around is chaos. As leaders working with teens, we often find ourselves in the same position—peacemaker in the midst of chaos. Most of us feel ill-equipped or inadequate for the job.

In Ambrose we find a person who is faithful in a place of turmoil despite his own fears. In Christ and in our faith, we find one who is fully adequate and who gives us words and strength in the midst of a storm. Scripture tells us that God never disappoints those who have faith (*Ecclesiasticus 2:7-11*). God does not require perfection of faith, but a faithful heart that knows God will provide.

While these words are easy to say, they are much harder to live. As leaders of young people we need to show our own vulnerability and fears of being inadequate. Just as Ambrose felt inadequate for the work he was called to do, we must help young people understand that feelings of inadequacy in the life of faith are common. Despite our inadequacy and fear, God is graciously abundant in Christ and will provide the strength for each day.

> God of all wisdom and knowledge, give your blessing and guidance to all who teach in your Church, that by word and example they may lead those whom they teach to the knowledge and love of you; through Jesus Christ our Lord. Amen.
>
> For Catechists or Teachers
> *The Book of Occasional Services*, p. 167

Coming Together
(Time est: 10-15 min)

At the front of the room on a piece of newsprint, write words associated with the Church that many people often do not understand. For example: atonement, sanctification, collect, episcopate, rubrics. (Look in *The Book of Common Prayer* for additional words.)

Be sure you know the meaning of the words you select—use a dictionary of church terms if necessary. As the group gathers, ask each individual to write definitions of the words on the newsprint or on separate pieces of paper.

After everyone has gathered, ask the youth to find *Ecclesiasticus 2:7-11* in their Bibles. Select a lector to lead the following prayer (Session Leaflet, p. 2).

> **Lector:** Let us pray.
> Dear God,
> Forgive us our sins. Help us to persuade people in good and loving ways, instead of harmful ways. Help us to use our powers of persuasion for your good. Amen.
> Katy, grade 7

> **Lector:** A reading from Ecclesiasticus, chapter 2, verses 7 through 11.
> (Full text on p. 2)
> **Lector:** The Word of the Lord.
> **People:** Thanks be to God.

Engaging
(Time est: 15-20 min)

Ask the youth to look over or read aloud the definitions they wrote for the words in the Coming Together activity. Take a vote to determine the "best" or "favorite" definition for each word.

Tell the youth the story of Ambrose and explain why his life is important to the Church. Emphasize that although he was reluctant and unprepared to be a bishop, he used his skills as a mediator and peacemaker to bring Christ to others. His gift for teaching in plain words helped everyone understand the good news of the gospel.

Share with the group the "official" definitions of the words from the activity. In small groups, define each of the words in plainer, more approachable language. Share the definitions with the larger group.

- How does language affect the way we tell others about Jesus?
- Do you think "church" words sometimes act as barriers between people?
- Is there anything about the worship service at your church that you

would change to help you understand it better?

Optional Activities

The following activities offer groups a wide range of choices. Consider the interests and strengths of youth and leaders and select those activity options that seem best suited to local time and talents. Remember no one can do everything!

Expressions

- **Word crazy:** Ask the youth to share words and phrases that drive them crazy about adult speech. What words do teachers, parents, priests, coaches and others use that are confusing or complicated? How do you feel when you don't understand? Ask one of the youth to write the responses on one side of a piece of newsprint. Next to the responses, find words or phrases that could be used in the place of those that are objectionable. The youth could suggest these alternatives if appropriate.
- **Role play:** Reenact this scene between an adult and young person: An adult asks a teen to do something using words or a phrase that make no sense to the teen. Act out his or her frustration and how to ask for clarification. How do we make people communicate clearly with us without getting angry or walking away? Act out other scenes showing ways to confront people that are both positive and negative, such as a discussion about curfew, homework, and television.
- **Other than words:** Ask the group to find ways other than words to express ourselves. Choices might include music, dance, mask making, face painting, and sign language. Divide into small groups to express one idea in scripture in different ways. For example, they could express the key verse in a variety of media.

Games

- **Talk show:** Youth can take turns being the host, audience, or guests on a talk show. Think of several situations, such as a confrontation between a strict parent and a child who just wants to have a little fun. Scenarios can be put in a hat and chosen at random. The youth should be able to demonstrate positive and negatives ways to convince others of their opinions, needs, convictions, and how to compromise. How can we make open conflict move towards understanding?

Media

Today's youth live in a media-rich culture that the Church cannot ignore. However, congregational norms about appropriate experiences vary and need to be respected. When choosing media activities consider local sentiments and prevailing laws covering public performances of copyrighted material.

- **Video:** Watch *Squanto*, a Disney movie about the Native American who acted as mediator for his people both in England and in this country.
- **Print:** Find several examples of conflict from newspapers during the week, or bring newspapers and ask youth to find appropriate stories. Let the group suggest "new endings" of stories by using mediation and clear language.

Music

Music is important for today's youth and can be an integral part of youth experience in the context of Bible and Church activities. The music suggestions offered here reflect a broad variety of possibilities from simple listening to hearty music making. Seek out musicians within youth, church, and community groups to sing and play along.

- Learn "The eternal gifts of Christ the King" (*The Hymnal 1982*, 234). The words were written by Ambrose.
- Listen to *Chant* or other religious chant music. Do you find the music soothing? When could you use this kind of music in your own life?
- Listen to "We Can Work It Out" by The Beatles. In what ways do the lyrics suggest that people resolve their differences?

WEAVINGS

- This session could be scheduled close to December 7, the day the Church recognizes Ambrose.
- The definition of eloquent includes words we might expect, such as fluent, aptness, and moving. However, eloquence is also defined as exhibiting "power" or characterized by "forcible" expression. Speakers who move us are more likely to use forceful language rather than flowery words.
- Sometimes people, like Ambrose, are called to be more eloquent, courageous, or patient than they thought they could be. The gawky Abraham Lincoln delivered the most moving tribute after the battle of Gettysburg. Journalists, professors, and others found reserves of deep spirituality when captured as hostages in Lebanon. Others for whom we have no names have performed courageous acts in times of war and disasters. With God's help, we all can tap into inner resources to meet times of crisis.

Service
- **Telling a story:** "Rewrite" several familiar Bible stories or folk tales in song, dance, or drama. Present the stories for children at a local day-care center or hospital or for the elderly at a senior center.
- **Peer counseling:** Find out about training in conflict resolution and peer counseling programs offered through schools and local agencies.

Sharing
- **Dictionary:** Compile a dictionary for new acolytes or new members that explains simple words like sanctuary, transept, or burse that are used in the church. The dictionary could also include confusing theological terms from *The Book of Common Prayer* and Bible that the group defined during the Engaging activity.

Study
- Read about conflict resolution in books such as the Channing L. Bete Co. Catalogue on Conflict Management and Resolution.
- Find out more about Augustine, Bishop of Hippo, in *Lesser Feasts and Fasts*, August 28. Ambrose was instrumental in the conversion of Augustine, possibly the greatest and most enduring theologian in Western Christianity.

Voices
Read and discuss the following quotations (Session Leaflet, p. 2).

> After the font [of baptism], the Holy Spirit is poured on you, the spirit of wisdom and understanding, the spirit of counsel and strength, the spirit of knowledge and godliness, and the spirit of holy fear.
> De Sacramentis 3.8

> Great talkers are so constituted that they do not know their own thoughts until, on the tide of their particular gift, they hear them issuing from their mouths.
> Thornton Wilder

> Were the works of God readily understandable by human reason, they would be neither wonderful nor unspeakable.
> Thomas à Kempis

Going Forth
Gather the group for a closing prayer and dismissal. Read together the prayer for Ambrose on his feast day December 7 in *Lesser Feasts and Fasts* (also on p. 3 of the Session Leaflet).

Leader: *Let us pray.*
O God, you gave your servant Ambrose grace eloquently to proclaim your righteousness in the great congregation, and fearlessly to bear reproach for the honor of your Name: Mercifully grant to all bishops and pastors such excellence in preaching and faithfulness in ministering your Word, that your people may be partakers with them of the glory that shall be revealed; through Jesus Christ our Lord, who lives and reigns with you and the Holy Spirit, one God, now and for ever. Amen.
Ambrose
Lesser Feasts and Fasts, December 7

Leader: *Let us go forth into the world, rejoicing in the power of the Spirit.*
People: *Thanks be to God.*

Look For
Can youth name ways that words can be effective in persuading other to change? Were they able to look for ways to use words to make an argument for their views? Are youth able to remain calm while articulating opposing ideas?

NOTES

Columba: Building Community
Called Through Faith

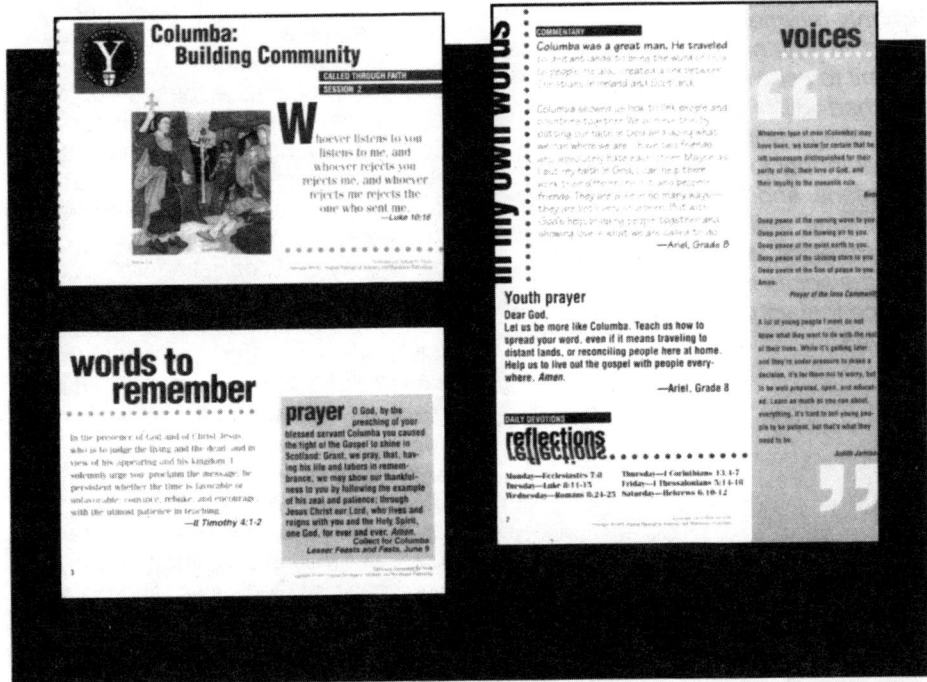

Objective
This session focuses on Columba, the founder of a monastic community in Iona, Scotland. The youth will be able to discuss how one person can make a difference in spreading the Christian message with patience and hard work. Youth will list ways they can bring Christ's message to people they see each day.

Background for Leaders
The Commentary tells about the life of Columba and his lessons in building community. The key person is Columba, and the key place is Iona off the coast of Scotland. For spiritual preparation contrast the way we live and how we preach the gospel.

Commentary
Columba is remembered for his missionary work of bringing the gospel of Christ to what is now present-day Scotland. Columba actually began his ministry in his native Ireland. Before his ordination to the priesthood at age 30, he had already founded monasteries at Derry and Durrow.

Columba was able to lead others to Christ by his gentle manner and his powerful preaching. He was committed to working closely with those he had trained as missionaries, and he never lost sight of the importance of life in community. Columba also helped to forge a relationship between the Irish and Scottish Churches by traveling to synods and encouraging lively exchange between communities.

Columba was given possession of the island of Iona which is off the coast of Scotland. As abbot he established a monastery that became a center for missionary training and evangelism. The monks of the Iona community often lived in little huts or beehive cells made out of mud and wattle that protected them from the elements and provided them with a safe place to pray.

Although their time was devoted to prayer, the monks welcomed all pilgrims with generous hospitality. For Columba, mission meant not only sharing the gospel but living with others and building community wherever he went.

Columba worked, studied and prayed wherever he went. He taught that the patience of daily work in community is as important as preaching and teaching. He died peacefully while making a copy of the Psalter.

For further study: Read more about Columba in *Lesser Feasts and Fasts*, June 9.

SESSION LEAFLET

■ **Art**—*Columba*, by Bobbi Tull

■ **Key Verse**—*Whoever listens to you listens to me, and whoever rejects you rejects me, and whoever rejects me rejects the one who sent me.*
—Luke 10:16

■ **Youth Commentary and Prayer**

■ **Voices**—Bede, Prayer of the Iona Community, Judith Jamison

■ **Daily Reflections**

■ **Words to Remember**

■ **Prayer**—Collect for Columba (*Lesser Feasts and Fasts*, June 9)

LECTOR'S TEXT

[Jesus said,] "Whoever listens to you listens to me, and whoever rejects you rejects me, and whoever rejects me rejects the one who sent me." The seventy returned with joy, saying, "Lord, in your name even the demons submit to us!" He said to them, "I watched Satan fall from heaven like a flash of lightening. See, I have given you authority to tread on snakes and scorpions, and over all the power of the enemy; and nothing will hurt you. Nevertheless, do not rejoice at this, that the spirits submit to you, but rejoice that your names are written in heaven."

Luke 10:16-20

TIPS ON THE TOPIC

- The youth may need you to help them find ways to include each person in the group in the Engaging activity. Working together in community means respecting each person's contributions.
- Helping youth to develop leadership skills is an important function of youth programs. If the group enjoys "teaching themselves," find ways to let them be in charge.
- **Discussion Starter:** What is one thing you can do to help the church community?

Personal Views

One of the great gifts that Columba gives us is the message that the quality and effect of our faith is measured as much by how we live as by what we preach. As a native person, I have encountered many zealous missionaries who want to spread the gospel. Too often, though, they scorn the people and the culture of those they want to reach. Sometimes, missionaries do not encourage these people to join them in spreading the gospel. Occasionally, missionaries misunderstand local customs and stay apart from the people they want to serve.

Columba shows us that building community and coexisting with people is essential to faithful mission work. For those of us whose mission is to work with youth, what does this mean? To be effective, we should not scorn the customs of those we serve. We should live and work side by side with those to whom we are called. That may not be easy with some young people who may seem foreign to us. But they are waiting to hear the good news of God's love. The gospel in action accepts them for who they are, where they come from, and trusts them to be leaders in community.

Think about your relationships with young people in your life. What parts of their life do you share? When is the last time you listened to their favorite music? Reflect on Columba and his example of living the good news.

Everliving God, whose will it is that all should come to you through your Son Jesus Christ: Inspire our witness to him, that all may know the power of his forgiveness and the hope of his resurrection; who lives and reigns with you and the Holy Spirit, one God, now and for ever. Amen.

For the Mission of the Church
The Book of Common Prayer, p. 816

Coming Together
(Time est: 10-15 min)

Hang Resource Poster No. 1 at the front of the room. The poster includes facts about Columba and symbols used by the Iona community. If the group is large, you may want to photo copy the fact sheet about Columba. If the Resource Poster is not available, write down on a large piece of paper, key facts about Columba from the Commentary, weavings, and material in *Lesser Feasts and Fasts,* June 9.

Ask the youth to read over the information while the group arrives. After everyone has gathered, ask the youth to find *Luke 10:16-20* in their Bibles. Select a lector to lead the following prayer (Session Leaflet, p. 2).

Lector: *Let us pray.*
Dear God,
Let us be more like Columba. Teach us how to spread your word, even if it means traveling to distant lands, or reconciling people here at home. Help us to live out the gospel with people everywhere. Amen.

Ariel, grade 8

Lector: *A reading from the Gospel of Luke, chapter 10, verses 16 through 20.*
(Full text on p. 2)
Lector: *The Word of the Lord.*
People: *Thanks be to God.*

Engaging
(Time est: 15-20 min)

Explain to the group that they will be teaching each other this week. Each person in the group has gifts and skills that are needed for ministry. As they learn from each other about Columba and his missions, they will also discover their gifts of ministry and what it means to be part of a community of faith.

Divide into small groups, if possible, and let the youth assign tasks according to their gifts and preferences. One group or person could look over the Commentary and the Columba fact sheet and decide how to share this information with the others. Another group could identify an art project to decorate the room that everyone could be a part of. A music group could find hymns or other music to create a mood for learning about Columba. Another group could discuss a service project that exemplifies Columba's message. The range of activities will depend on the size of the group and the diversity of their gifts.

- Do you like teaching yourselves?
- Did you work as a community or did one or two people do all the work?
- How did you include everyone in the group in planning and teaching the lesson?

Optional Activities

The following activities offer groups a wide range of choices. Consider the interests and strengths of youth and leaders and select those activity options that seem best suited to local time and talents. Remember no one can do everything!

Expressions

- **Prayer hut:** The Iona community that Columba founded built small prayer huts for protection against the elements and for private focus. These huts allowed them a small prayer sanctuary in the midst of a chaotic world. Construct prayer huts out of cardboard boxes or put blankets over chairs. Give each person time to be alone in one of the "prayer huts."
- **Shrine:** Create a small shrine of paper or other material with symbols that help you think about God. Place the shrine in a private place at home to signify that place as a "prayer hut."
- **Prayer:** Ask the group to write a brief prayer that captures a common concern or need. Make a covenant with each other to say the prayer each day at a particular time for at least a week.

Games

- **Shake hands:** Before playing the game, tell one youth without the others seeing that he or she is the "Columba." Tell the group that Columba has joined your midst to form a community. The only way to tell if you have encountered Columba or a convert is by a handshake which is followed by a light squeeze of the hand. Ask the group to begin circulating around the room, shaking each others hands. When you receive the special handshake, you can begin spreading it yourself!

Media

Today's youth live in a media-rich culture that the Church cannot ignore. However, congregational norms about appropriate experiences vary and need to be respected. When choosing media activities consider local sentiments and prevailing laws covering public performances of copyrighted material.

- **Video:** Watch *The Secret of Roan Innish* about forming a community.
- **Print:** Illustrate the dictionary described in the Sharing activity by taking pictures at your church. The altar guild can help the group photograph things used in the Eucharist and altar hangings from different seasons.

Music

Music is important for today's youth and can be an integral part of youth experience in the context of Bible and Church activities. The music suggestions offered here reflect a broad variety of possibilities from simple listening to hearty music making. Seek out musicians within youth, church, and community groups to sing and play along.

- Listen to the music of "The King of love my shepherd is" (*The Hymnal 1982*, 645), written by Columba. Make a mosaic reflection of the hymn using pens and marker. Use the mosaic at home in your "prayer hut," or display them at your church.
- Sing "Here I Am, Lord" (*Glory and Praise*, Vol. 3, 198). How did Columba hold the people in his heart?
- Listen to any album by the Chieftains, an Irish folk band.

Service

- **Beating the bounds:** It is customary on the northern isles of Great Britain to walk the boundary of the parish. This is called "beating the bounds." Walk around an area or neighborhood surrounding the church while keeping your eyes open for specific needs of the community. At particular places, the group should stop, build a "cairn" (a stacking of six to eight small stones), and pray silently. Use the prayer composed for the Expressions activity.

WEAVINGS

- Schedule this session sometime before Columba's feast day on June 9 to give the youth time to plan a coffee hour treat for the parish.
- Columba is often associated with a pet crane that is said to have followed him faithfully. However, the symbol of the Iona community found through the island is a wild goose, symbolizing the call to go wherever God's spirit leads us.
- Columba's example as a missionary is as valid today as it was in Scotland in the sixth century. Too often in the past, missionary zeal obscured the love that God has for all people. The conquerors of the New World, for example, often used religion as an excuse to murder or enslave native peoples. Even today, we sometimes run roughshod over the culture and people we are trying to reach with the good news of the gospel. Only by working together as Columba did, can we build enduring communities of faith.

- Columba Facts and Symbols (No. 1)

RESOURCE POSTER

Sharing

■ **Hospitality:** Welcoming others is essential in building community and developing leadership skills. Make oatmeal cookies, shortbread, or another Scottish treat to share with the entire community at coffee hour. The mosaics made for the Music activity could be displayed, and youth could share information about Columba.

Study

■ **Patrick:** Patrick of Ireland is said to have foretold Columba's birth in a prophecy. Look up Columba in *Lesser Feasts and Fasts,* June 9, and read the words attributed to Patrick. Find out more about this Irish saint by reading his story in *Lesser Feasts and Fasts,* March 17.

■ **Iona:** Look up the island of Iona on a map and read about the area. If you visited Iona today, the community of faith is very evident. Find out what the symbol of the wild goose means to the community.

Voices

Read and discuss the following quotations (Session Leaflet, p. 2).

Whatever type of man [Columba] may have been, we know for certain that he left successors distinguished for their purity of life, their love of God, and their loyalty to the monastic rule.
Bede

Deep peace
of the running wave to you.
Deep peace
of the flowing air to you.
Deep peace
of the quiet earth to you.
Deep peace
of the shining stars to you.
Deep peace
of the Son of peace to you. Amen.
    Prayer of the Iona Community

A lot of young people I meet do not know what they want to do with the rest of their lives. While it's getting later and they're under pressure to make a decision, it's for them not to worry, but to be well prepared, open, and educated. Learn as much as you can about everything. It's hard to tell young people to be patient, but that's what they need to be.
Judith Jamison

NOTES

Going Forth

Gather the group for a closing prayer and dismissal. Read together Collect for Columba in *Lesser Feasts and Fasts,* June 9 (also on p. 3 of the Session Leaflet).

Leader: *Let us pray.*
O God, by the preaching of your blessed servant Columba you caused the light of the Gospel to shine in Scotland: Grant, we pray, that, having his life and labors in remembrance, we may show our thankfulness to you by following the example of his zeal and patience; through Jesus Christ our Lord, who lives and reigns with you and the Holy Spirit, one God, for ever and ever. Amen.
    Collect for Columba
    Lesser Feasts and Fasts, June 9

Leader: *Let us go forth into the world, rejoicing in the power of the Spirit.*
People: *Thanks be to God.*

Look For

Can the youth use Columba's ideas about community in working as a group? Are they able to see the importance of patience and hard work in spreading the Christian message? Can the youth list ways they can bring Christ's message to people they see each day?

Thomas à Becket: Choosing God
Called Through Faith

Objective

This session focuses on Thomas à Becket, archbishop of Canterbury, who was slain in 1170. Youth will discuss the difficulties of discerning which "things" should be given to the government and which "things" are God's. They will draft criteria for making decisions and exploring priorities.

Background for Leaders

The Commentary is about Thomas à Becket's falling out with his friend King Henry II. Key people are Becket, Archbishop Theobald, and King Henry II; key places are England and the Canterbury Cathedral. For spiritual preparation think making choices that reflect our Christian beliefs.

Commentary

Thomas à Becket was one of the more famous archbishops of Canterbury in England. He was well-educated and came from a Norman family of the ruling class. Becket studied in Paris but lack of finances forced his return to England. He worked as a notary until being assigned in 1142 to the then archbishop of Canterbury, Theobald, who arranged for Becket to study in Bologna. Becket was ordained a deacon in 1154 when he became archdeacon of Canterbury.

Later as chancellor he became good friends with King Henry II. Becket was considered the second most influential man in the kingdom because of this friendship. Becket felt he could be truthful with Henry because they were such close friends and often traveled and hunted together.

Henry insisted that Becket become archbishop when Theobald died. Although Becket told the king he did not want to accept the post, he was consecrated as archbishop in 1162.

Shortly after his consecration, his relationship with the king became strained over many issues. His unwillingness to swear unreserved obedience to the king angered Henry. However, Becket knew that making such an oath violated law of the church.

Becket fled England in 1164 in search of support from Pope Alexander III who refused to interfere on his behalf. When he returned to England, he was murdered by a band of armed men in Canterbury Cathedral. Although King Henry probably had nothing to do with the death of Becket, the public outcry forced him to publicly honor Becket. Henry built a shrine to Thomas in Canterbury Cathedral, made a pilgrimage, and did penance at the site.

SESSION LEAFLET

■ **Art**—*Thomas à Becket*, by Bobbi Tull

■ **Key Verse**—Jesus said to them, "Give to the emperor the things that are the emperor's, and to God the things that are God's."
—Mark 12:17a

■ **Youth Commentary and Prayer**

■ **Voices**—Thomas à Becket, Lord Melbourne, Leo Tolstoy, Robert Boyd Munger

■ **Daily Reflections**

■ **Words to Remember**

■ **Prayer**—For those who suffer for the sake of Conscience (BCP, p. 823)

Episcopal Curriculum for Youth—Called Through Faith
Copyright © 1997 Virginia Theological Seminary and Morehouse Publishing

LECTOR'S TEXT

Then they sent to him some Pharisees and some Herodians to trap him in what he said. And they came and said to him, "Teacher, we know that you are sincere, and show deference to no one; for you do not regard people with partiality, but teach the way of God in accordance with truth. Is it lawful to pay taxes to the emperor, or not? Should we pay them, or should we not?" But knowing their hypocrisy, he said to them, "Why are you putting me to the test? Bring me a denarius and let me see it." And they brought one. Then he said to them, "Whose head is this, and whose title?" They answered, "The emperor's." Jesus said to them, "Give to the emperor the things that are the emperor's, and to God the things that are God's." And they were utterly amazed at him.

Mark 12:13-17

TIPS ON THE TOPIC

- The Engaging activity may result in disagreements among youth. Be prepared to help them confront each other in appropriate ways.
- Youth find going against a friend to be very difficult. However, there are times that friends make us do things we know are wrong. Help the youth find ways to stand up to their friend when necessary.
- **Discussion Starter:** Has a friend ever asked you to do something you know is wrong? What did you do?

Personal Views

We can only wonder how a gentle, brilliant and faithful person such as Becket might get himself into such a conflict with someone as powerful as a king. Each of us, though not faced with kings, is often confronted by powers that strongly urge us to do something in violation of our faith.

Adults struggle with the concept of separation of Church and state. Young people struggle with the powerful politics of their peers. What will we sacrifice to be cool and accepted? What will we sacrifice to keep our beliefs?

Life is filled with choices, and often we are overwhelmed by the complexity and consequences of our choices. To choose between God and king, power and justice, also means that we may lose friends, position, and sometimes our freedom.

Thomas à Becket provides us with a model of living a faithful life in the midst of a monumental corrupting power. No one would blame Becket, even today, if he had gone along with Henry in order to keep peace and stay alive. The relationship he had with Henry was brotherly—they were well-matched companions who enjoyed life together. Becket was forced to choose between the comfort and familiarity of his relationship with Henry and the convictions he held for God.

Close friends can be honest with one another, but sometimes that same honesty can drive people apart forever. The lesson we learn from Becket is that even beyond death God is a God of justice.

God calls us to take responsibility in all that we do, and to act faithfully despite pressures from government, peers, or kings. Despite losing his life, Becket stands as an example of one who has conquered the fear of death to experience the true joy of serving a just God. Who are the "kings" in your life that keep you from God? Does your loyalty to certain friends stand between you and God?

Almighty God, you proclaim your truth in every age by many voices: Direct, in our time, we pray, those who speak where many listen and write what many read; that they may do their part in making the heart of this people wise, its mind sound, and its will righteous; to the honor of Jesus Christ our Lord. Amen.

For those who Influence Public Opinion
The Book of Common Prayer, p. 827

Coming Together
(Time est: 10-15 min)

On one side of the room, hang a piece of blue construction paper. On the other side, hang a piece of red paper. As the youth enter, tell them to choose to sit on either the blue or red side of the room. Don't provide any additional guidance.

After everyone has gathered, ask the youth to find *Mark 12:13-17* in their Bibles. Select a lector to lead the following prayer (Session Leaflet, p. 2).

Lector: *Let us pray.*
Dear God,
We pray that we will be able to tell the difference between what is yours and what belongs to the government. We would like to have the strength to be able to make the right decision. Please give us the confidence to do so. Amen.

Kristin, grade 7

Lector: *A reading from the Gospel of Mark, chapter 12, verses 13 through 17.*

(Full text on p. 2)

Lector: *The Word of the Lord.*
People: *Thanks be to God.*

Engaging
(Time est: 15-20 min)

Ask the group to explain the reasons they chose to sit on the blue or red side. Explain that the session today is about making choices that can be as easy as picking out a place to sit or as difficult as going against a friend.

Tell the story of Thomas à Becket using information from the commentary. Spend some time reflecting on the relationship between Henry and Thomas. Show Resource Poster No. 2 of the interior of a cathedral. Note the lack of pews: at the time of Becket, people met in cathedrals not only to worship, but also to conduct business and to socialize.

Divide the room into four areas, each designated with a different sign: "Tell an Authority," "Do Nothing," "Confront the Thief," and "Tell the Owner." The leader will describe a specific scenario. Each person will decide which of the four signs best describes his or her response to each situation, and then move to that area of the room. Each person should be prepared to explain his or her rationale after each move. Stop and discuss the rationales after each scenario.

Use the following situations or create your own:
- You saw someone steal something.
- Your best friend is the thief.
- Your best friend owned the item that is stolen.
- The item stolen belongs to your mother.
- The item stolen is a pencil.
- The item stolen is a computer.
- The item is stolen from your school.
- The item is taken from your church.
- The thief is hungry and the item is food.

Discuss how choices are made and how we can be influenced by others.

Optional Activities

The following activities offer groups a wide range of choices. Consider the interests and strengths of youth and leaders and select those activity options that seem best suited to local time and talents. Remember no one can do everything!

Expressions
- **Role play:** Dramatize a confrontation between friends or peers. Encourage youth to create scenes that depict actual situations. Work in small groups and share the dramas.
- **Painting:** Create a group poster using only fingerpaints. Use your hands to express the confusing and profound emotions found in relationships and with friends. During the activity, ask the youth to be silent, communicating only with their hands. Is the poster a community effort or an amalgamation of separate expressions?

Games
- Do you know me? Ask the youth to make up three statements to describe themselves, two of which are true, and one that is false. For example: I have two cats; my mother is from Ireland; and our car is green. Take turns telling the statements. After each person finishes, the group must determine the false statement. Continue until everyone has played. How can you tell when someone isn't telling the truth? How do we confront a friend who isn't telling the truth?

Media
Today's youth live in a media-rich culture that the Church cannot ignore. However, congregational norms about appropriate experiences vary and need to be respected. When choosing media activities consider local sentiments and prevailing laws covering public performances of copyrighted material.
- **Video:** Watch selected scenes from the movie *Becket*. What scene shows the dilemma Becket faced in confronting his friend Henry?
- **Print:** Get several copies of the play *Murder in the Cathedral* by T. S. Eliot. Look up the last scene and ask the youth to describe the way they picture it. Do you think Henry had anything to do with Becket's death?

Music
Music is important for today's youth and can be an integral part of youth experience in the context of Bible and Church activities. The music suggestions offered here reflect a broad variety of possibilities from simple listening to hearty music making. Seek out musicians within youth, church, and community groups to sing and play along.
- Look up "All who love and serve your city" (*The Hymnal 1982*, 571).
- Sing "Be Not Afraid" (*Gather*, GIA Publications, Inc., 430).
- Listen to "Think" by Aretha Franklin.

WEAVINGS
- This session could be scheduled close to All Saints Day. Although Becket does not have an official feast day, his life manifests the saints' "virtuous and godly living" (All Saints' Day, BCP, p. 245).
- As adults, we have discovered many "gray" areas in our lives. Often, choices involve complex and overlapping issues in which there are no clear answers. Before you judge choices made by others too harshly, think about your own conflicting dilemmas.
- During times of civil war and strife, people who otherwise would be friends find themselves as enemies. During the American Civil War, sometimes even families found themselves on opposite sides. More recently, our country was divided over the Vietnam conflict. Today neighbors are pitted against each other in this and other countries like Ireland, Serbia, Bosnia, and Sudan. Pray for people who live in the midst of conflict.

RESOURCE POSTER
- Interior of a Gothic Cathedral (No. 2)

Service

■ **Hard choices:** Gather information about different charities, such as Church World Services, the Children's Defense Fund, and the Presiding Bishop's Fund for World Relief. Discuss the goals of different organizations and select one that the group will support. Find a way to raise money through a group fund raiser.

Sharing

■ **Counseling:** Propose that the vestry design a parish-based peer counseling program for youth and younger children. List reasons why a counseling program would be beneficial and encourage the vestry to include youth in the planning process.

Study

■ **Reading:** Learn more about Thomas à Becket's life by reading T. S. Eliot's *Murder in the Cathedral*. You can also read portions of Chaucer's *Canterbury Tales* which describe the pilgrimages made to the shrine of Thomas à Becket.

■ **Art:** At the library, look up different writers' and artists' depictions of the life of Thomas à Becket. Compare them with scenes you imagined when you heard the story.

Voices

Read and discuss the following quotations (Session Leaflet, p. 2).

I had to choose between God and you, sir. I chose God.
    Thomas à Becket

Nobody ever did anything very foolish except from some strong principle.
    Lord Melbourne

It is easier to produce ten volumes of philosophical writings than to put one principle into practice.
    Leo Tolstoy

Christianity is the power of God in the soul of [a person].
    Robert Boyd Munger

Going Forth

Gather the group for a closing prayer and dismissal. Read together the prayer on page 823 of The Book of Common Prayer (also on p. 3 of the Session Leaflet).

Leader: *Let us pray.*
O God our father, whose Son forgave his enemies while he was suffering shame and death: Strengthen those who suffer for the sake of conscience; when they are accused, save them from speaking in hate; when they are rejected, save them from bitterness; when they are imprisoned, save them from despair; and to us your servants, give grace to respect their witness and to discern the truth, that our society may be cleansed and strengthened. This we ask for the sake of Jesus Christ, our merciful and righteous Judge. Amen.
    For those who suffer for the sake of Conscience
    The Book of Common Prayer, p. 823

Leader: *Let us go forth into the world, rejoicing in the power of the Spirit.*
People: *Thanks be to God.*

Look For

Are youth able to describe which things belong to government and which things belong to God? Can they set priorities for making decisions? Do they recognize the effect other people have on their choices?

NOTES

Joan of Arc: Soldier for Christ
Called through Faith

Objective

The focus of this session is Joan of Arc and her unwavering devotion to God. Youth will be able to discuss the difficulty of listening to a voice that is counter to the prevailing culture. They will name ways they can live their faith in a world filled with obstacles.

Background for Leaders

The Commentary describes the life of Joan of Arc and her example of courage. Key people are Joan, King Charles, and Saints Michael, Catherine, and Margaret; the key event is the Hundred Years' War in France. For spiritual preparation, think about how to listen to God when facing difficult choices.

Commentary

Joan of Arc, also known as the Maid of Orleans, was born into a rural peasant farming family in France in the early part of the fifteenth century. No one could have guessed that this simple girl could so dramatically change the course of western civilization, not only in a political sense, but also in terms of its religious outlook—and all at the tender age of sixteen. This unsophisticated peasant girl successfully led the army of France in battle against the English in the Hundred Years' War, symbolizing not only a startling military prowess but also a faithful persistence and courage for millions of people who have admired her since.

Inspired by the voices of Saints Michael, Catherine and Margaret, Joan of Arc claimed at an early age to have been blessed with an unique and direct line of communication with God. She claimed to have a strong and unshakable understanding of God's will for France. Her vision, which called for the expulsion of the menacing English presence from French soil and the coronation of Charles, the rightful heir to the French throne, led her to offer her assistance to Charles' army. Not surprisingly, the girl was rebuffed and strictly examined by the Church hierarchy for signs of insanity and unorthodox beliefs. She was sent home. She later returned and was able to convince Charles that her plan not only served his purposes, but God's as well.

Joan donned the clothing of her fellow soldiers and defeated the English under her own standard and banner. Her vision and persistence won the day, and she stood at Charles' side for his coronation as king.

A year later, as she protected the rear guard of her army in retreat, the English captured Joan with the aid of French collaborators. No one came to her rescue, and when her captors realized that neither threat nor torture would compel her to recant, she was burned at the stake as a heretic. Her life is celebrated not only for these

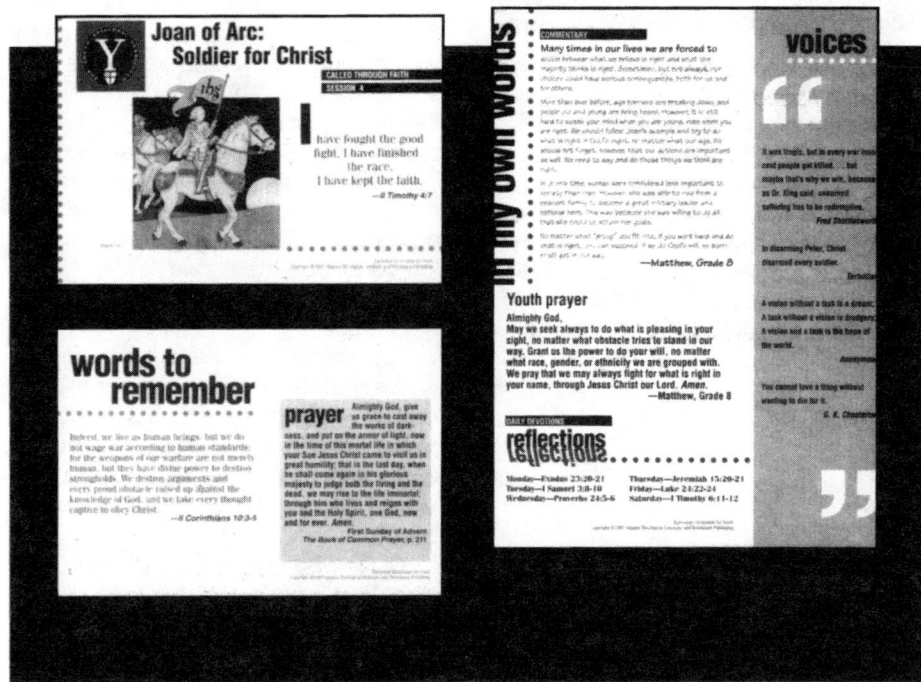

SESSION LEAFLET

■ **Art**—*Joan of Arc*, by Bobbi Tull

■ **Key Verse**—*I have fought the good fight, I have finished the race, I have kept the faith.*
—II Timothy 4:7

■ **Youth Commentary and Prayer**

■ **Voices**—Fred Shuttlesworth, Tertullian, Anonymous, G. K. Chesterton

■ **Daily Reflections**

■ **Words to Remember**

■ **Prayer**—First Sunday of Advent (BCP, p. 211)

LECTOR'S TEXT

As for me, I am already being poured out as a libation, and the time of my departure has come. I have fought the good fight, I have finished the race, I have kept the faith. From now on there is reserved for me the crown of righteousness, which the Lord, the righteous judge, will give me on that day, and not only to me but also to all who have longed for his appearing.

II Timothy 4:6-8

TIPS ON THE TOPIC

- Be prepared to address the issue of cults and heeding voices that do not come from God. Invite youth to set their own criteria for judging the "authentic" voice of God.
- Youth may wonder why God called Joan to war instead of peace. Stress that she followed her heart and remained true to the voice she heard there.
- **Discussion Starter:** Have you ever felt called to do something that is unpopular? What did you do?

heroic achievements, but also for her deep trust in God. She remains to this day a symbol of unity and an example of courage in crisis for the people of France and of the world.

Personal Views

Most of us will never have to face the challenges and endure the lonely suffering of the extremely young Joan of Arc. And yet, we find ourselves in situations where our faith is tested by those who would have us act differently from the ways we believe to be right. It is much easier to do the right thing when those around you are in agreement. When we are alone and forced to face the crowd, we can understand what it must have been like for Joan.

Joan's faith was fueled by a genuine sense of God's call to her in the voices of the saints. The Bible offers many ways in which God communicates with us. Do we listen for that voice? Do we always like what we hear?

Quite often we are tempted to deny that "little voice" inside of us that calls us to do God's will. What are some of the current choices you are facing? How do you weigh the risks involved as you seek to make the right choice?

Upon her capture by the English, how disheartening it must have been for Joan to be abandoned by those she had helped. What sustained and supported her when her choices were to deny her visionary experience of God or to die? What are the things that sustain you when you feel called to make an unpopular choice?

Save us from weak resignation to the evils we deplore; let the gift of thy salvation be our glory evermore. Grant us wisdom, grant us courage, serving thee whom we adore, serving thee whom we adore.

God of grace and God of glory
The Hymnal 1982, 594

Coming Together
(Time est: 10-15 min)

Make a graffiti poster header by writing the sentence: "I'd rather DIE than _____." Put markers, pens, and crayons next to the poster. As youth enter, ask them to complete the sentence on the poster by writing their own endings. Don't provide any more direction.

After everyone has gathered, ask the youth to find *II Timothy 4:6-8* in their Bibles. Select a lector to lead the following prayer (Session Leaflet, p. 2).

Lector: *Let us pray.*
Almighty God,
May we seek always to do what is pleasing in your sight, no matter what obstacle tries to stand in our way. Grant us the power to do your will, no matter what race, gender, or ethnicity we are grouped with. We pray that we may always fight for what is right in your name, through Jesus Christ our Lord. Amen.

Matthew, Grade 8

Lector: *A reading from II Timothy, chapter 4, verses 6 through 8.*
(Full text on p. 2)
Lector: *The Word of the Lord.*
People: *Thanks be to God.*

Engaging
(Time est: 15-20 min)

Ask the youth if they have ever used the phrase from the Coming Together activity. Discuss the responses on the graffiti board, and mark the ones that are worth dying for.

Find out how much information the youth already know about Joan of Arc. Display Resource Poster No. 3 of Joan at her retreat at Vauculeurs. From facts in the Commentary, tell the story of Joan. See if your facts differ from the youth's information. How did Joan hear God's commands?

Divide the youth into two groups, and ask one group to line up facing the other group to form pairs. One person from the first group will describe a personal dilemma that he or she makes up or gets from the graffiti poster. The person facing him or her responds as the "voice of God." Discuss the dilemma and response.

- Does God ever speak directly to us?
- How do we know if the message we get came from God?

- How can you "hear" the voice of God outside of church?
- Who can help you make an unpopular but important choice?

Optional Activities

The following activities offer groups a wide range of choices. Consider the interests and strengths of youth and leaders and select those activity options that seem best suited to local time and talents. Remember no one can do everything!

Expressions

- **Drama:** Write a dramatic play or scene about Joan of Arc, or fictionalize the character and place her in a modern setting. (Refer to Resource Poster No. 3) Think about the setting—would it be in another country, such as Ireland or Bosnia, or closer to home? Do you want to show her talking to the saints, on the battlefield, questioned by the authorities, or another scene?
- **Standards:** Bring in paint, markers, cardboard or paper, and scissors. Ask a youth to read *Ephesians 6:13-14.* Point out that Joan led the army of France under her own standard and banner. Decorate your own shield and banner with Christian symbols that best represent you.
- **Journaling:** Write a private journal entry about a time when you thought you were "losing it," when you thought you were going crazy, or you were not understood or accepted. What did you do? Who was most helpful?

Games

- **God's Armies:** Divide the group into two armies, one led by Joan and the other led by the English. Ask each "army" to line up, shoulder to shoulder, facing the other "army." The first person from one side (with help from the other "soldiers") must describe a person in history or current events who did great things as a very young person or very old person. The first person on the next side, responds in similar fashion. The game continues, with the next people in line describing an old or young person. The game is over when both sides are stumped.

Media

Today's youth live in a media-rich culture that the Church cannot ignore. However, congregational norms about appropriate experiences vary and need to be respected. When choosing media activities consider local sentiments and prevailing laws covering public performances of copyrighted material.

- **Video:** Watch *Oh God* and discuss the funny and engaging way in which George Burns portrays God. At a longer session, watch the original movie production of *Joan of Arc,* starring Ingrid Bergman.
- **Print:** Look through copies of magazines for young people, such as *National Geographic World* and *Discover,* about young people who have stood up for what they believed.

Music

Music is important for today's youth and can be an integral part of youth experience in the context of Bible and Church activities. The music suggestions offered here reflect a broad variety of possibilities from simple listening to hearty music making. Seek out musicians within youth, church, and community groups to sing and play along.

- Sing or read "God of grace and God of glory" (*The Hymnal 1982,* 594). What does it say about God's presence in the midst of our dilemmas?
- Sing "Trust in the Lord" (*Glory and Praise* Vol. 2, 151). What renews courage and helps us "soar with eagle's might"?
- Listen to "What if God Was One of Us?" by Crash Test Dummies, and discuss the questions the lyrics raise.

Service

- **Take action:** Identify a local or national issue that is important to the group. Take action by finding out who has power and influence over decisions affecting this issue. Write letters, send e-mail, or make phone calls expressing your views.

WEAVINGS

- A heretic is defined as a believer who holds religious opinions that are contrary to those accepted by the Church or as someone who rejects the doctrines of the Church. The word is derived from a Greek word that means able to choose. Joan was branded as a heretic by Church leaders who expected her to deny the voices in her heart and embrace their doctrine.
- Joan of Arc is a reminder that a person's age does not determine their ability as leaders or visionaries. Alexander the Great was leading armies to conquer far away lands when he was still in his twenties. Many of the patriots that led this country politically and on the battlefield during the Revolutionary War were also very young. Sarah was well past child-bearing age when God told Abraham that his and Sarah's offspring would be as numerous as the stars in the sky. Mary, the mother of Jesus, was still a teenager when she was visited by the angel Gabriel. God can call anyone at any time.

RESOURCE POSTER

- Saint Joan of Arc in Her Retreat at Vauculeurs (No. 3)

Sharing
- **On stage:** Present the play written for the Expressions activity to the parish or to a younger group of children. Bring the shields and banners made by youth to decorate the room.

Study
- **Peace:** Look up the list of Nobel Peace Prize winners in the *World Almanac*. Select one and learn about his or her life, work, and motivation to answer the call of peace. Do your research at a library or on the Internet.
- **Unpopular choices:** Look through one of the Gospels or a book about people in the Bible. Identify those who made unpopular choices. What did they have in common?
- **War:** Find out about the Hundred Years' War fought between France and England. What were the major issues? If you had lived at that time, would you have supported King Charles?

Voices
Read and discuss the following quotations (Session Leaflet, p. 2).

It was tragic, but in every war innocent people get killed. . . but maybe that's why we win, because as Dr. King said, unearned suffering has to be redemptive.
— Fred Shuttlesworth

In disarming Peter, Christ disarmed every soldier.
— Tertullian

A vision without a task is a dream;
A task without a vision is drudgery;
A vision and a task is the hope of the world.
— Anonymous

You cannot love a thing without wanting to die for it.
— G. K. Chesterton

NOTES

Going Forth
Gather the group for a closing prayer and dismissal. Read together the prayer on page 211 of *The Book of Common Prayer* (also on p. 3 of the Session Leaflet).

Leader: *Let us pray.*
Almighty God, give us grace to cast away the works of darkness, and put on the armor of light, now in the time of this mortal life in which your Son Jesus Christ came to visit us in great humility; that in the last day, when he shall come again in his glorious majesty to judge both the living and the dead, we may rise to the life immortal; through him who lives and reigns with you and the Holy Spirit, one God, now and for ever. Amen.
First Sunday of Advent
The Book of Common Prayer, p. 211

Leader: *Let us go forth into the world, rejoicing in the power of the Spirit.*
People: *Thanks be to God.*

Look For
Are youth able to discuss the difficulty of listening to a voice that seems to be counter to their culture? Can they name ways they can live their faith in a world filled with obstacles?

Thomas Cranmer: Building on a Foundation
Called through Faith

Objective
The focus of this session is the life of Thomas Cranmer and his efforts to reform the Church. Youth will discuss the ways individuals have influenced the reform of worship, doctrine, and practice of the Church. They will identify changes they could make that would improve Church and society.

Background for Leaders
The Commentary looks at the way Thomas Cranmer sought to change the Church by building on a foundation laid by others. Key people are Thomas Cranmer, Nicholas Ridley, Hugh Latimer, and King Henry VIII; the key event is the establishment of the Church of England. For spiritual preparation, think about how the Church has changed to make the Gospel more widely available.

Commentary
Efforts at reforming the worship, doctrine and practice of the Church have not always been easy, nor have they always been peaceful. Indeed, they have at times been painful for the community. They have sometimes been fatal for those caught in the midst of controversy. Thomas Cranmer, along with followers Nicholas Ridley and Hugh Latimer, stands in a long line of people who heard God's call. They built upon the foundation of the Church's history and tradition in new and often challenging ways.

In the English Church, Thomas Cranmer played a principal role in providing an accessible way for all the people of England to experience scripture, worship, and private prayer in their own language.

Writing in English instead of Latin, he developed the first *Book of Common Prayer* in 1549, and its subsequent revision in 1552. His efforts at reforming the Church, altered the course of the Church for all time.

Thomas Cranmer's influence was not limited to the Church alone. His ultimate belief that God's will demanded the King's predominance in all things political and religious led Cranmer into many disagreements. The foremost of these was the crisis of the annulment of King Henry VIII's marriage to his first wife, Catherine of Aragon. Cranmer was appointed Archbishop of Canterbury in 1533, and at the king's request, declared the marriage void. This action, along with religious reforms which appeared to dilute the power of the pope, would forever brand Cranmer as an enemy of Rome. Indeed, his mixed loyalty to crown and Church would one day cost him his life.

After Henry's death, a crisis arose regarding the proper succession to the throne. The new queen, Mary, a Roman Catholic, ordered Cranmer's death by burning. While Cranmer wrote several denials of his earlier beliefs while in prison, he ultimately held fast to his principles. Before he

SESSION LEAFLET

■ **Art**—*Thomas Cranmer*, by Bobbi Tull

■ **Key Verse**—*According to the grace of God given to me, like a skilled master builder I laid a foundation, and someone else is building on it. Each builder must choose with care how to build on it.*
—I Corinthians 3:10

■ **Youth Commentary and Prayer**

■ **Voices**—Alfred North Whitehead, H. R. Buckle, Calvin Coolidge, English Proverb

■ **Daily Reflections**

■ **Words to Remember**

■ **Prayer**—Collect for Hugh Latimer, Nicholas Ridley, and Thomas Cranmer (*Lesser Feasts and Fasts*, October 16)

Episcopal Curriculum for Youth—Called Through Faith
Copyright © 1997 Virginia Theological Seminary and Morehouse Publishing

LECTOR'S TEXT

For we are God's servants, working together; you are God's field, God's building. According to the grace of God given to me, like a skilled master builder I laid a foundation, and someone else is building on it. Each builder must choose with care how to build on it. For no one can lay any foundation other than the one that has been laid; that foundation is Jesus Christ. Now if anyone builds on the foundation with gold, silver, precious stones, wood, hay, straw—the work of each builder will become visible, for the Day will disclose it, because it will be revealed with fire, and the fire will test what sort of work each has done. If what has been built on the foundation survives, the builder will receive a reward.

I Corinthians 3:9-14

TIPS ON THE TOPIC

- Youth may want to talk about what the Church will look like in the next century. Be open to looking ahead in time and space at the Church of the Future.
- Youth may be fascinated by the way Cranmer died by being burned at the stake. Don't get sidetracked from his important contributions as archbishop and his willingness to die for his beliefs.
- **Discussion Starter:** What is one thing you could do to put a newcomer at ease?

died he thrust his hand into the fire, saying, "for as much as my hand offended in writing contrary to my heart, therefore my hand shall be punished first; for if I may come to the fire, it shall first be burned."

For further study: Read about Cranmer, Latimer, and Ridley in *Lesser Feasts and Fasts* on their Feast Day, October 16.

Personal Views

While the Church today struggles with many different and some times divisive issues, it is hard to imagine a predicament like Thomas Cranmer's in which a prominent archbishop is given the choice to deny his beliefs or die in the fire. Rarely are Church leaders in our country today directly confronted with choosing between their loyalty to the nation and Church. The goals of reform about which Cranmer cared so deeply and for which he was willing to risk so much can still raise relevant issues for us today.

Accessibility, both physical and social, in a highly diverse community can be an emotional issue. Often those who are "inside" and those who are left "outside" of a particular group or institution have difficulty understanding each other's point of view and experience. Hurt feelings can polarize communities of people to where they believe they have less in common than is actually the case. Can you recall a time when you were the one outside looking in? What feelings surface with such memories?

Thomas Cranmer made changes and reforms in Church structure and practice that put out a "welcome mat" for more and more people. With his artfully named Book of "Common" Prayer, he sought to draw more people into the church so that regardless of our differences, we would all worship the Lord together, in common. The process of gracefully adapting tradition and doctrine so that the people's worship of God might more clearly and accurately reflect the authentic words of God's people continues to this day.

How firm a foundation, ye saints of the Lord, is laid for your faith in his excellent word! What more can he say than to you he hath said, to you that for refuge to Jesus have fled?

How firm a foundation
The Hymnal 1982, 636

Coming Together
(Time est: 10-15 min)

At the front of the room hang a large piece of newsprint with the words: Signs of Welcome. As youth enter, ask them to write or draw the things they encounter in their community, at their school, among their friends, or at their church that make them feel welcome. Encourage them to think of both physical and social signs that make these places accessible, such as open doors and friendly smiles.

Next to the sign, hang another piece of newsprint with the words: Not Welcome. Ask youth to write or draw things that repel or discourage them from feeling welcome, such as locked doors or rude looks.

After everyone has gathered, ask the youth to find I Corinthians 3:9-14 in their Bibles. Select a lector to lead the following prayer (Session Leaflet, p. 2).

Lector: *Let us pray.*
Dear God, we ask you to give us strength to do your will. We ask you to make us servants of your peace, and to give us courage to do what is right in our hearts and in your sight. Also, we ask you to help us to be kind and forgiving to others who have strayed from your path. Amen.

Peter, Grade 7

Lector: *A reading from I Corinthians, chapter 3, verses 9 through 14.*

(Full text on p. 2)
Lector: *The Word of the Lord.*
People: *Thanks be to God.*

Engaging
(Time est: 15-20 min)

Discuss the entries on the welcome and unwelcome posters. Encourage youth to share stories about times they felt welcome or unwelcome and what made them feel this way. Explore their reactions to those feelings.

- Was it difficult to return to a place you felt unwelcome?
- What "sign" put you immediately at ease?
- How do you welcome newcomers to the church or your school?

Retell the story of Thomas Cranmer who sought, at the expense of his life, to open worship to all of God's people. The Church teaches that the Bible, tradition (the history and practice of the Church's experience) and reason (our ability as children of God to seek and find God's will) are the three basic building blocks of the Church. Cranmer used these as the foundation for his work in building up the Church.

Draw a brick wall with three large blocks at the foundation labeled Bible, Tradition, and Reason. Ask youth to fill in the blank bricks with the other important aspects of the Church's life, such as Outreach, Family, Community, or Forgiveness.
- Which blocks do you feel are most important?
- What would the Church be like if we took away some of the blocks?

Optional Activities

The following activities offer groups a wide range of choices. Consider the interests and strengths of youth and leaders and select those activity options that seem best suited to local time and talents. Remember no one can do everything!

Expressions
- **Welcome:** Draw a sign or make a mat for your room that would help people feel welcome. Use words from the Coming Together activity or create images that are welcoming.
- **Prayers:** Write in your own words a prayer from *The Book of Common Prayer*, such as the Collect for Ordination, p. 540. Explore the powerful images presented in this prayer, then "reform" its language so that friends who don't come to this church can understand its meaning.

Games
- **Shoes:** Ask the group to remove their shoes and place the left shoe in one pile and the right shoe in another. Either redistribute the shoes randomly or let the youth close their eyes and choose one from each pile. Be sure no one has his or her own shoes or a matching pair. If possible, let them try the shoes on and walk a bit to experience a pair of shoes that doesn't fit. Then, ask them to match the shoes with their mates <u>without</u> taking the shoes off. Place matching pairs together, right shoe by left, until every shoe has its mate next to it, regardless as to who is wearing which shoe.

Media

Today's youth live in a media-rich culture that the Church cannot ignore. However, congregational norms about appropriate experiences vary and need to be respected. When choosing media activities consider local sentiments and prevailing laws covering public performances of copyrighted material.
- **Video:** Watch a portion of "The Six Wives of Henry VIII," a PBS series that describes the political and religious controversies of the day.
- **Print:** Bring in several sets of newspapers. Randomly pick stories form the sports, business, and editorial sections. Compare words and phrases from the different sections. Is the style of writing different? Identify words or phrases that people who rarely read those sections might not understand. How could you change it?

Music

Music is important for today's youth and can be an integral part of youth experience in the context of Bible and Church activities. The music suggestions offered here reflect a broad variety of possibilities from simple listening to hearty music making. Seek out musicians within youth, church, and community groups to sing and play along.
- Read the words of "How firm a foundation" (*The Hymnal 1982*, 636). How does God help us in times of trouble?
- Sing "Within Our Darkest Night" (*Gather*, GIA Publications, Inc.,

WEAVINGS
- Schedule this session close to Cranmer's Feast Day on October 16. It could also be coupled with Session 5 of the module on The Episcopal Church Year that deals with the lectionary.
- One of Cranmer's great contributions was the creation of the lectionary, the schedule by which almost all of the Bible, New and Old Testaments, is read before the people. The Lectionary for Sundays provides a focal point for preaching and teaching in the Episcopal Church. Find out more about the lectionary in *The Book of Common Prayer,* beginning on p. 888.
- The "new" *Book of Common Prayer* in the 1970's caused a great deal of concern in the Episcopal Church. Some people felt that the beauty of the language in the 1928 prayer book had been lost while others found the 1979 book to be more expressive of their faith. The changes made in worship in 1549 with the publication of Cranmer's *Book of Common Prayer* were much more revolutionary. By writing a *Book of "Common" Prayer*, he took control of worship from the priests and gave it to the people. The changes in language were also radical, moving from Latin, which could be understood by an elite few, to "common" English. Pray that our Church will continue to build on the foundation of scripture, tradition, and reason, welcoming all those who seek Christ.

456). Think about Cranmer's darkest night and how he faced his fears.
- Listen to "When You Walk Through a Storm" from the musical *Carousel*. Write an additional verse or new lyrics.

Service
- **Worship:** Design a worship service for people who aren't Episcopalian and have no other church experience. You may want to use the Order of Celebrating the Holy Eucharist (BCP, p. 401-402) or design another liturgy. Present the service at a nursing home or other setting.

Sharing
- **Opening the church:** One of Cranmer's goals was making people feel welcome in church. What could be changed to make your church welcoming to more people? Be sure to address concrete issues such as handicapped parking, ramps, and language and liturgical barriers. Present your ideas to the those responsible for worship.

Study
- **Feast day:** Read the entry in *Lesser Feasts and Fasts* for October 16, the feast day for Cranmer, Latimer, and Ridley. Find out more about their lives and why they share this day.
- **Prayer books:** Since Cranmer's first edition in 1549, there have been many updated versions of *The Book of Common Prayer*. Find out how many versions have been written, and what major changes were made.

Voices
Read and discuss the following quotations (Session Leaflet, p. 2).

The worship of God is not a rule of safety—it is an adventure of the spirit, a flight after the unattainable.
    Alfred North Whitehead

Almost every reform consists in the clearing away of an old rather than in the making of a new law.
    H. R. Buckle

It is only when [people] begin to worship that they begin to grow.
    Calvin Coolidge

It is not the suffering but the cause which makes a martyr.
    English Proverb

Going Forth
Gather the group for a closing prayer and dismissal. Read together the collect for October 16 in *Lesser Feasts and Fasts* (also on p. 3 of the Session Leaflet).

> **Leader:** *Let us pray.*
> *Keep us, O Lord, constant in faith and zealous in witness, that, like your servants, Hugh Latimer, Nicholas Ridley, and Thomas Cranmer, we may live in your fear, die in your favor, and rest in your peace; for the sake of Jesus Christ your Son our Lord, who lives and reigns with you and the Holy Spirit, one God, now and for ever. Amen*
>   Collect for Hugh Latimer, Nicholas Ridley, and Thomas Cranmer
>   *Lesser Feasts and Fasts*, October 16

> **Leader:** *Let us go forth into the world, rejoicing in the power of the Spirit.*
> **People:** *Thanks be to God.*

Look For
Are youth able to name ways people have influenced the reform of worship and doctrines in the Church? Can they identify changes they could make that would improve their church and society?

NOTES

Robert Raikes: Teaching the Gospel
Called through Faith

Objective
The focus of this session is the work of Robert Raikes who started the first Sunday School. Youth will discuss how knowledge can be a powerful weapon against ignorance and inexperience. They will be able to list ways they might teach others about God's message of love and hope.

Background for Leaders
The Commentary is about Robert Raikes' concern for children and their knowledge about God. The key event is the founding of the first Sunday Schools; the key place is England during the industrial revolution. For spiritual preparation reflect on your own Sunday School experiences and how they affected your life.

Commentary
The educational experience of the average child in Robert Raikes' time was vastly different from that of most children in today's world. In the mid-eighteenth century England experienced a vast industrial development which demanded a growing work force. Many families, desperate for resources and driven from farms into the cities in search of work, had no choice but to place their children in factories and sweatshops to earn enough money for the family to survive. Most of these children worked six days a week and went without even the most basic elements of an education.

In these difficult circumstances, Robert Raikes conceived of an alternative for working children and their families. Raikes, a well-to-do journalist and philanthropist who had devoted much of his attention to the issue of prison reform in England, devised a plan that would satisfy two important needs. Each child would have access to supervised education in a supportive and caring environment that would benefit all of society. He also reasoned that a well-educated, morally-sound population was less likely to engage in "a life of crime." Through the establishment of parish schools that would teach children reading and church doctrine, these two goals could be met.

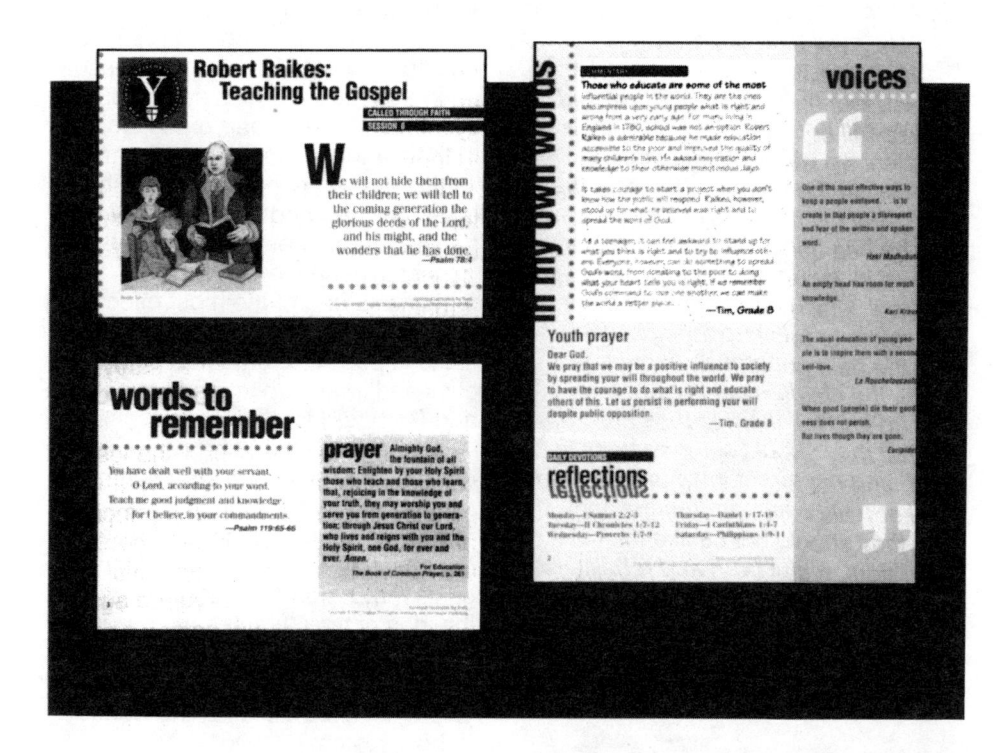

Raikes' efforts were not unopposed. Opponents argued that these schools resulted in an inappropriate observance of the Sabbath day. They saw little need for educating poor children. But Raikes and the parish churches persisted. The first of many "Sunday Schools" (Sunday being the only non-working day for most children and parents) was established in 1780, with lay women as teachers who often used their own homes for classrooms. Raikes himself drew the interest of children through simple object lessons designed to illustrate theological ideas.

In just a short time, the Sunday School system had become so successful that Raikes was able to report

SESSION LEAFLET

■ **Art**—*Robert Raikes*, by Bobbi Tull

■ **Key Verse**—*We will not hide them from their children; we will tell to the coming generation the glorious deeds of the Lord, and his might, and the wonders that he has done.*
—Psalm 78:4

■ **Youth Commentary and Prayer**

■ **Voices**—Haki Madhubuti, Karl Kraus, La Rouchefoucauld, Euripides

■ **Daily Reflections**

■ **Words to Remember**

■ **Prayer**—For Education (BCP, p. 261)

LECTOR'S TEXT

Give ear, O my people, to my teaching; incline your ears to the words of my mouth. I will open my mouth in a parable; I will utter dark sayings from of old, things that we have heard and known, that our ancestors have told us. We will not hide them from their children; we will tell to the coming generation the glorious deeds of the Lord, and his might, and the wonders that he has done. He established a decree in Jacob, and appointed a law in Israel, which he commanded our ancestors to teach to their children; that the next generation might know them, the children yet unborn, and rise up and tell them to their children, so that they should set their hope in God, and not forget the works of God, but keep his commandments; and that they should not be like their ancestors, a stubborn and rebellious generation, a generation whose heart was not steadfast, whose spirit was not faithful to God.

Psalm 78:1-8

TIPS ON THE TOPIC

- You may need to describe a "sweatshop" and the working conditions faced by the children Raikes wanted to reach. If youth want to know more about this period, suggest they read books by Charles Dickens or others.
- The use of everyday objects is an important part of this session. Begin collecting random objects early in the week in a sack in your kitchen, office, or bedroom. Ask other family members to help you.
- **Discussion Starter:** What is your best memory about Sunday School?

---

in his newspaper, the *Gloucester Journal*, that his district was "quite a heaven on Sundays." By Raikes' death it was estimated that over 500,000 children were participating in this exciting educational undertaking.

Personal Views

What began for Robert Raikes as an effort to help his community resulted in a vastly influential educational system and the spread of the Gospel to thousands of families in England. To this day, we expect the Church to teach children and adults alike. While people's memories of their Sunday School experience may vary, it remains as one of the most effective and consistent opportunities for all kinds of people to gather to study, discuss and reflect upon God's Word and God's will for their lives.

Although the world has changed considerably since the eighteenth century, not all the founding principles of Raikes' original Sunday Schools are obsolete. While Raikes' initial goals may belong to a bygone age, the idea of the Church setting aside Sunday as a special time for study as well as worship survives. What motivated you to be a part of the Sunday School system?

The ideal Christian education, as Raikes perceived it, not only familiarized the learner with the doctrine and the tradition of the faith, but also equipped God's people to act as moral beings in a confusing and sinful world. Only a people who understand God's requirements can be expected and prepared to do what is right in God's sight. How has your Sunday School experience affected the decisions you make?

Our present world can be considered no less confusing, nor less sinful than Raikes'. We all are constantly bombarded with conflicting messages to alter our values. Youth are increasingly asked to make decisions that children growing up a generation ago never faced. Imagine the shape of today's society, locally or on a greater scale, without a foundation of Christian principles to guide and support us.

Almighty God, heavenly Father, you have blessed us with the joy and care of children: Give us calm strength and patient wisdom as we bring them up, that we may teach them to love whatever is just and true and good, following the example of our Savior Jesus Christ. *Amen.*

For the Care of Children
The Book of Common Prayer, p. 829

Coming Together
(Time est: 10-15 min)

Bring several refrigerator magnets and some small metal objects, such as paper clips, pins, and nails. Scatter the magnets and objects on a table in the center of the room. As youth enter, encourage them to play with the magnets.

After everyone has gathered, ask the youth to find *Psalm 78:1-8* in their Bibles. Select a lector to lead the following prayer (Session Leaflet, p. 2).

Lector: *Let us pray.*
Dear God,
We pray that we may be a positive influence to society by spreading your will throughout the world. We pray to have the courage to do what is right and educate others of this. Let us persist in performing your will despite public opposition.

Tim, Grade 7

Lector: *A reading from Psalms, chapter 78, verses 1 through 8.*
(Full text on p. 2)

Lector: *The Word of the Lord.*
People: *Thanks be to God.*

Engaging
(Time est: 15-20 min)

Display Resource Poster No. 4 showing Robert Raikes with a group of children. Tell the story of Raikes and his hopes for the children of his times. Focus on his simple but effective use of everyday objects such as the magnet and the pins to illustrate important lessons from the Bible. (Read about the use of magnets and pins in the Weavings section.)

Ask youth to pair up. Give each pair one everyday household object, such as a ball of string, a can opener, hammer, or anything you find around the house. Ask them to relate the

object to a Bible story or person. If possible, provide enough Bibles and books with Bible stories or about people in the Bible for each pair.
- Was it difficult to find a story about your object?
- How did Jesus teach people? Think about the stories and parables he told.
- What is it about simple objects that makes them a powerful teaching tool?
- Do stories and objects help you learn?
- How could you use an object to tell a friend something important? What would that object be?

Optional Activities

The following activities offer groups a wide range of choices. Consider the interests and strengths of youth and leaders and select those activity options that seem best suited to local time and talents. Remember no one can do everything!

Expressions
- **Sculpture:** Bring in small, insignificant objects such as bits of string, cotton balls, small pieces of fabric, paper clips, and buttons. Using all of the items, create a group sculpture of a biblical scene or story. Be sure to provide glue and tape to help the creative process.
- **We Want You!** Using paints, markers, and poster board, create posters to recruit Sunday School teachers or youth workers. To help youth with ideas, provide copies of curriculum materials used by your church. Focus on positive images and words that would attract people to participate.

Games
- **Charades:** Divide the class into teams and provide each team with a variety of small everyday items (kitchen, household, or office) and a passage from Scripture in which Jesus tells a parable. Each team must act out the parable using each of the items they have been given as props. The other teams must guess the parable.
- **Games of the times:** Young people living at this time did not have sophisticated games and sports equipment that we have today. They played games with found objects, such as sticks and stones. Design a game using found objects in your room or an outdoor area.

Media
Today's youth live in a media-rich culture that the Church cannot ignore. However, congregational norms about appropriate experiences vary and need to be respected. When choosing media activities consider local sentiments and prevailing laws covering public performances of copyrighted material.
- **Video:** Watch *Stand and Deliver* and discuss how the efforts of one teacher changed the lives of so many students. What lessons did they learn besides calculus?
- **Print:** Collect examples of other Sunday School materials, either used in the parish by other age groups or from other parishes or denominations. Ask youth to evaluate differences between the materials and identify the goals of each.

Music
Music is important for today's youth and can be an integral part of youth experience in the context of Bible and Church activities. The music suggestions offered here reflect a broad variety of possibilities from simple listening to hearty music making. Seek out musicians within youth, church, and community groups to sing and play along.
- Read or sing "O Zion, haste, thy mission high fulfilling" (*The Hymnal 1982*, 539) or "Book of books, our people's strength" (631).
- Sing "Christ the Worker" (*Songs for Celebration*, H-298).
- Listen to "I Believe the Children Are Our Future" by Whitney Houston or "Teach Your Children" by Crosby, Stills, Nash and Young.

Service
- **Materials:** Collect Sunday School materials or Bibles that are unused or in good condition and send them to overseas missions, area churches or companion parishes in need. Contact the National Church's Office of Children's Ministries or the

WEAVINGS

- Schedule this session before Sunday School registration or teacher recruitment at your church.
- Robert Raikes was known for drawing theological ideas from simple objects. He used this skill to spark children's interest in the Gospel. In one instance, Raikes drew a magnet across a table covered in pins like those produced by the children in the local factory. Having caught the children's attention and interest, he explained that the Gospel was like the magnet, attracting and leading followers in new and exciting ways. How can you use simple objects to draw youth closer to God?
- The sweatshops depicted by authors such as Charles Dickens no longer dominate urban England. However, child labor is still used in many developing nations. Children are expected to support their families by working long hours in conditions that are less than ideal. Even in our county, some businesses, such as the garment industry, place workers, who are often immigrants, in conditions that can only be described as sweatshops. Pray for workers throughout the world whose jobs cause misery and pain.

RESOURCE POSTER

- Drawing Children to God (No. 4)

local diocesan office for suggestions.

Sharing

- **Bible School:** Volunteer to assist at Vacation Bible School or a special education event in the parish.
- **Teaching:** Prepare and teach a Bible story to younger children in the parish using simple objects or the sculpture made for the Expressions activity.

Study

- **History:** Gather information on the progress of the Sunday School movement worldwide and in other denominations. How are the movements similar? How are they different?
- **At Home:** Investigate the history of your own parish Sunday School by looking through church records and interviewing education leaders, present and past. Have there been changes in the education program that mirrored changes in the life of the parish? Write a report of your findings for the church newsletter.
- **Family:** Interview a parent or grandparent about their Sunday School experience. How is it similar to yours? How is it different?

Voices

Read and discuss the following quotations (Session Leaflet, p. 2).

One of the most effective ways to keep a people enslaved. . . is to create in that people a disrespect and fear of the written and spoken word.
Haki Madhubuti

An empty head has room for much knowledge.
Karl Kraus

The usual education of young people is to inspire them with a second self-love.
La Rouchefoucauld

When good [people] die their goodness does not perish,
But lives though they are gone.
Euripides

Going Forth

Gather the group for a closing prayer and dismissal. Read together the prayer on page 261 of *The Book of Common Prayer* (also on p. 3 of the Session Leaflet).

Leader: *Let us pray.*
Almighty God, the fountain of all wisdom: Enlighten by your Holy Spirit those who teach and those who learn, that, rejoicing in the knowledge of your truth, they may worship you and serve you from generation to generation; through Jesus Christ our Lord, who lives and reigns with you and the Holy Spirit, one God, for ever and ever. Amen.
For Education
The Book of Common Prayer, p. 261

Leader: *Let us go forth into the world, rejoicing in the power of the Spirit.*
People: *Thanks be to God.*

Look For

Are youth able to discuss the importance of knowledge? Can they name ways knowledge can be used against ignorance and inexperience? Youth will be able to list ways they can teach others.

NOTES

Amy Carmichael: Saving the Poor
Called through Faith

Objective
This session centers on the life of missionary Amy Carmichael. Youth will be able to name different ways people can be poor and to discuss how they can be more aware of poverty in their midst. They will list ways they can help people living in poverty.

Background for Leaders
The Commentary looks at the life of Amy Carmichael and her call to service. Key people are Amy Carmichael and "shawlies;" key places are Belfast, Ireland, and Bangalore, India. For spiritual preparation, think about your response to God's call.

Commentary
Amy Carmichael spent most of her life working with the poor, embracing the poorest of the poor as her own. Born in Northern Ireland on December 16, 1867, Carmichael was the rambunctious oldest child of a Scottish flour miller. The ring leader of her seven siblings, Amy Carmichael was from the beginning a risk-taker. She recalled giving each of her siblings a bit of poison just for fun, to see how long it would take them to die!

She later wrote that as an adolescent she was anything but religious. But at 17 she and her two brothers had an experience that would change the course of her life and open up in her a deep spirituality. The three youth were walking through the streets of Belfast when they came upon an old woman dressed in rags and struggling with a large bundle. They were drawn to help her, even though they felt embarrassed to be seen with such a poor person. Carmichael never forgot that moment. By helping the woman she discovered what is really important—not gold or silver or what someone thinks. She spent the rest of her life living and working with the poor.

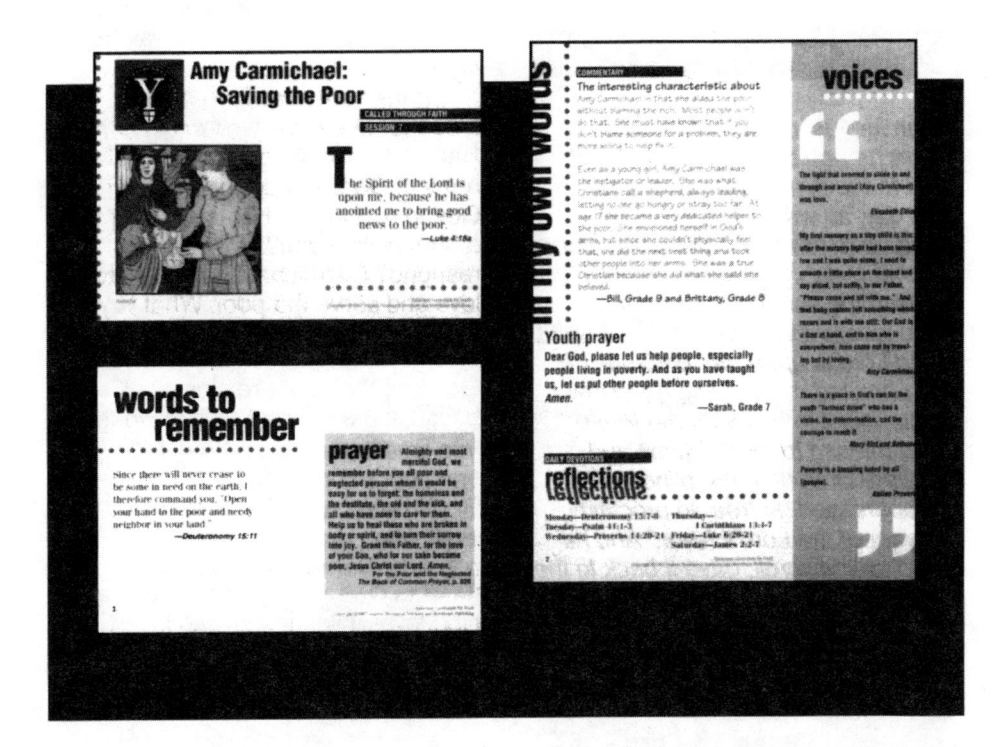

Carmichael began a fellowship with young women in Ireland who were too poor to even have a hat, and, therefore, were called "shawlies," because they wrapped their heads in their shawls. She led the women in Bible studies, helping them learn to read, as well as offering counseling and a place to gather. Eventually the ministry grew so large that a benefactor built them a hall called "The Welcome," big enough to seat 500.

But the impoverished streets of Bangalore, India called Carmichael away from her home, and there she served girls and boys who were being used as prostitutes. She built an orphanage, classrooms, a House of Prayer, and a hospital.

She was called "Amma" (the Tamil word for mother) by five generations of abandoned children. A prolific writer, Carmichael also wrote thirty-six books.

SESSION LEAFLET

■ **Art**—*Amy Carmichael*, by Bobbi Tull

■ **Key Verse**—*The Spirit of the Lord is upon me, because he has anointed me to bring good news to the poor.*
—Luke 4:18a

■ **Youth Commentary and Prayer**

■ **Voices**—Amy Carmichael, Elisabeth Elliot, Mary McLeod Bethune, Italian Proverb

■ **Daily Reflections**

■ **Words to Remember**

■ **Prayer**—For the Poor and the Neglected (BCP, p. 826)

LECTOR'S TEXT

When [Jesus] came to Nazareth, where he had been brought up, he went to the synagogue on the sabbath day, as was his custom. He stood up to read, and the scroll of the prophet Isaiah was given to him. He unrolled the scroll and found the place where it was written: "The Spirit of the Lord is upon me, because he has anointed me to bring good news to the poor. He has sent me to proclaim release to the captives and recovery of sight to the blind, to let the oppressed go free, to proclaim the year of the Lord's favor." And he rolled up the scroll, gave it back to the attendant, and sat down. The eyes of all in the synagogue were fixed on him. Then he began to say to them, "Today this scripture has been fulfilled in your hearing."

Luke 4:16-21

TIPS ON THE TOPIC

- Youth may believe poverty is the result of weakness or poor character. Help them understand that most people don't choose to be poor.
- Many people have never experienced true poverty first hand. Ask the youth to identify "necessities" they take for granted, such as food at the end of the month, a washing machine, or a family car. These are luxuries for the poor.
- **Discussion Starter:** What is one thing you could do for someone who is poor?

Personal Views

Amy Carmichael was out-going, loving, and vigilant about being selfless. Blessed with a warm and engaging personality, she committed her life to drawing people to Christ rather than to herself. Her resolve is amazing; surely she struggled with loneliness by living so far away from home.

Carmichael reports that as a teenager she felt a turn within herself. Rather than looking to nestle in the arms of God, she opened herself for God to rest in her. Have you ever felt a "turn" within you? How did you respond? Carmichael felt called to love and serve the poor. What is your call?

The witness of Jesus portrays that God and the poor are closely allied, because the heart of God is where true wealth resides. Both rich people and poor people are bound up in God's heart, and God values people even when most of the world does not. Amy Carmichael opened her heart to God, letting herself love as God loves. Like Jesus, she loved scandalously, both the rich and the poor.

O Lord, you have taught us that without love whatever we do is worth nothing: Send your Holy Spirit and pour into our hearts your greatest gift, which is love, the true bond of peace and of all virtue, without which whoever lives is accounted dead before you. Grant this for the sake of your only Son Jesus Christ, who lives and reigns with you and the Holy Spirit, one God, now and for ever. *Amen.*

7th Sunday after the Epiphany
The Book of Common Prayer, p. 216

Coming Together
(Time est: 10-15 min)

Bring in a special snack and a container filled with slips of paper of different colors. As the youth enter, ask them to select a piece of paper without looking. What they receive as a snack depends on the color of the paper. For example, red means they get a drink and two cookies; pink, only a drink; yellow, two cookies; green, one cookie; white, nothing.

Do not comment on the experience at first; just let the group deal with the situation. If asked, you might say, "I don't decide who gets a snack." Be prepared to share your observations later with the group. Did anyone offer to share their snack with someone who had none?

After everyone has gathered, ask the youth to find *Luke 4:16-21* in their Bibles. Select a lector to lead the following prayer (Session Leaflet, p. 2).

Lector: *Let us pray.*
Dear God, please let us help people, especially people living in poverty. And as you have taught us, let us put other people before ourselves. Amen.

Sarah, Grade 7

Lector: *A reading from the Gospel of Luke, chapter 4, verses 16 through 21.*

(Full text on p. 2)
Lector: *The Word of the Lord.*
People: *Thanks be to God.*

Engaging
(Time est: 15-20 min)

Tell the story of Amy Carmichael in your own words. Be sure to mention that Carmichael first embraced poor people at home before being called to a ministry in a foreign country.

Discuss the Coming Together experience in light of the scripture reading and the story of Amy Carmichael's life. Share your observations. Use the following questions to guide your discussion:

- How did you feel about being treated so differently?
- Does God make people rich or poor?
- What is our responsibility to share in poverty and wealth?
- How does what one person have affect what another has? Are resources unlimited?
- Why do some people have so much more than others?
- Amy Carmichael became poor by choosing to live and work with poor children. What is the difference between poverty of choice and poverty of circumstance?
- Why would someone choose to be poor?

Optional Activities

The following activities offer groups a wide range of choices. Consider the interests and strengths of youth and leaders and select those activity options that seem best suited to local time and talents. Remember no one can do everything!

Expressions

- **Shawlies:** Ask the youth to imagine they are among the shawlies that Amy Carmichael helped. As she leaves for India, several decide to write her a letter using skills she taught them. Ask the youth to compose a letter individually or as a group that will comfort Carmichael in her new home.
- **Color of poverty:** Put a large pile of crayons with many colors in the center of a table. Ask youth to pick out the colors they associate with poverty. Next, select the ones they associate with wealth. Now imagine yourself walking through a middle class neighborhood. What colors do you see on the houses? Now, mentally "walk" through a poorer neighborhood or a market place in a developing nation. What colors did you see: Look back at the first choices the group made about the color of poverty. Would you change the colors you associated with poverty or wealth?

Games

- **Relay race:** In two or more piles, place clothes for a complete outfit. In half of the piles, include clothes that look professional, sporty, or chic; in the other piles put clothes that are more clearly cast-off. With the "cast-off" piles, place an odd assortment of extra stuff in large garbage bags. Divide the youth by the number of piles of clothing. Racing against the clock and each other, one youth from each group will quickly dress, carry a fragile object across the room, race back, and tag the next youth in the group. Those in cast-off clothing also have to carry the garbage bag across the room. The game is over when everyone has had a turn. How did it feel for some of you to have the extra burden of your "life's belongings"?

Media

Today's youth live in a media-rich culture that the Church cannot ignore. However, congregational norms about appropriate experiences vary and need to be respected. When choosing media activities consider local sentiments and prevailing laws covering public performances of copyrighted material.

- **Video:** Watch the scene in *Little Women* in which the family, poor themselves, take their Christmas breakfast to immigrants who have nothing. Did everyone in the family willingly participate? How did they feel later?
- **Print:** It is possible to find Jesus in people around us every day. Look in news magazines for photographs of "Jesus" embracing the poor.

Music

Music is important for today's youth and can be an integral part of youth experience in the context of Bible and Church activities. The music suggestions offered here reflect a broad variety of possibilities from simple listening to hearty music making. Seek out musicians within youth, church, and community groups to sing and play along.

- Read or sing together "In your mercy, Lord, you called me," (*The Hymnal 1982*, 706). The lyrics recall Carmichael's "turn" as a teenager, when she opened her heart to God.
- Sing "Jesu, Jesu, fill us with your love" (*Hymns III*, H-213). Who were Amy Carmichael's neighbors?
- Listen to "Uptown Girl" by Billy Joel about the struggle with having the right stuff or coming from the "good" side of town.

Service

- **Close to home:** Recalling that Carmichael was first called to ministry near her home in Belfast, ask the youth to look for poverty that is close to home. Interview local social service personnel or contact a near-by welfare agency to get information. What are the areas of greatest poverty within a ten-mile radius of the parish? Decide how to respond to a specific need by gathering clothes for a rummage sale,

WEAVINGS

- This session could be scheduled near Amy Carmichael's birthday in December to coincide with the "baby shower" described in the Sharing option.
- The poor women of Belfast in Amy Carmichael's time were labeled "shawlies" because they wore shawls over their heads instead of scarves. In Russia, the women who wear similar scarves over their heads are called "babushkas," the Russian word for scarf. In the United States, poor women who carry their personal belongings with them, usually in garbage bags, are called "bag ladies." Labeling a group of people depersonalizes them and makes it easier for others to ignore their plight. What other terms are used to belittle the problems of the poor?
- When asked to describe Amy Carmichael, her friends and colleagues often used the word "love." Her biographer noted that "there is hardly a page of her books that does not speak of [love] in some way" (Elisabeth Elliot). Amy Carmichael found love in the faces of poverty. Where can you find love?

collecting canned goods for a local food pantry, or other outreach ministry.

Sharing
- **Baby shower:** After completing the survey on poverty close to the church, enlist the parish's assistance for the service project you selected. During the Christmas season, consider having a shower for the baby Jesus; contact a shelter or agency that serves children, and find out what is needed. Publish the list and ask the parish to bring the shower gifts, presenting them as part of a Sunday liturgy.

Study
- **Bible study:** Look through the *Gospel of Luke* to find the type of people Jesus spent time with. Many are poor in one way or another. What does Jesus's example say to us?
- **Untouchables:** Read *Deep River* by Japanese author Endo. The book tells of a Roman Catholic monk who follows the teaching of Jesus by carrying the corpses of impoverished, Indian untouchables to the Ganges River, a place of blessing.
- **Biography:** Read more about Amy Carmichael in *Bright Legacy: Portraits of Ten Outstanding Christian Women* by Elisabeth Elliot.

Voices
Read and discuss the following quotations (Session Leaflet, p. 2).

The light that seemed to shine in and through and around [Amy Carmichael] was love.
      Elisabeth Elliot

My first memory as a tiny child is this: after the nursery light had been turned low and I was quite alone, I used to smooth a little place on the sheet, and say aloud, but softly, to our Father, "Please come and sit with me." And that baby custom left something which recurs and is still with me still. Our God is a God at hand, and to him who is everywhere, men come not by travelling but by loving.
      Amy Carmichael

There is a place in God's sun for the youth "farthest down" who has a vision, the determination, and the courage to reach it.
      Mary McLeod Bethune

Poverty is a blessing hated by all [people].
      Italian Proverb

Going Forth
Gather the group for a closing prayer and dismissal. Read together the prayer on page 826 of *The Book of Common Prayer* (also on p. 3 of the Session Leaflet).

Leader: *Let us pray. Almighty and most merciful God, we remember before you all poor and neglected persons whom it would be easy for us to forget: the homeless and the destitute, the old and the sick, and all who have none to care for them. Help us to heal those who are broken in body or spirit, and to turn their sorrow into joy. Grant this, Father, for the love of your Son, who for our sake became poor, Jesus Christ our Lord. Amen.*
    For the Poor and the Neglected
    The Book of Common Prayer, p. 826

Leader: *Let us go forth into the world, rejoicing in the power of the Spirit.*
People: *Thanks be to God.*

Look For
Are youth able to relate to the life of this extraordinary missionary? Are they able to name different ways people can be poor. Are youth able to discuss how they can be more aware of poverty close to home? Can they list ways they can help people in poverty?

NOTES

Dietrich Bonhoeffer: Facing Evil
Called through Faith

Objective

The focus of the session is the witness of Dietrich Bonhoeffer to a life of faith and courage. Youth will be able to discuss the role of the Christian community in facing evil in the world. They will list ways that personal prayer, worship, everyday work, and Christian service can help them when confronted by evil.

Background for Leaders

The Commentary briefly describes the life and witness of Dietrich Bonhoeffer. Key people are Bonhoeffer and Frank Fisher; key groups are Jewish people in Germany and the German Confessing Church; the key event is the Holocaust. For spiritual preparation, think about how you individually and the Church face evil today.

Commentary

Dietrich Bonhoeffer, a Lutheran pastor and theologian, was born in Breslau, Germany in 1906. Trained in Germany, Bonhoeffer also spent a formative year studying at Union Theological Seminary in New York City. There in 1930 he met Frank Fisher, an African-American divinity student, who introduced Bonhoeffer to the blight of racism in the United States. Deeply influenced by their friendship, Bonhoeffer expressed moral outrage about the treatment of Jews back in his own country, leading ultimately to his death by hanging at Flossenburg concentration camp.

In 1933, as a teacher of theology at Berlin University in Germany, Bonhoeffer began protesting the anti-Jewish laws that were being forced upon the state, the university, and the Church. For protection he left Germany for a while and served as minister to a German congregation in London. Returning home in 1935, he became the head of a theological college founded by the anti-Nazi German Confessing Church. Because it was a threat to the Nazi regime, friends arranged a lecture tour back at Union Seminary for Bonhoeffer whose life was in danger. But Bonhoeffer would stay away from Germany only a few weeks. He felt compelled to re-join his fellow Christians in Nazi Germany and share the struggle of the Confessing Church.

Silenced by the government in 1939, Bonhoeffer joined the resistance movement and worked through his fellow clergy and others to enlist the Allies to cooperate against Adolph Hitler. Arrested by the Gestapo on April 5, 1943, Bonhoeffer was first imprisoned in Berlin, and later placed in concentration camps at Buchenwald and Flossenburg. During his imprisonment, he wrote a series of articles that continue to inspire Christians throughout the world. While in prison Bonhoeffer participated in an attempt to assassinate Hitler.

SESSION LEAFLET

■ **Art**—*Dietrich Bonhoeffer*, by Bobbi Tull

■ **Key Verse**—*The face of the Lord is against evildoers, to cut off the remembrance of them from the earth.*
—Psalms 34:16

■ **Youth Commentary and Prayer**

■ **Voices**—Dietrich Bonhoeffer, George Washington Carver, Edmund Burke

■ **Daily Reflections**

■ **Words to Remember**

■ **Prayer**—For Social Justice (BCP, p. 823)

LECTOR'S TEXT

Come, O children, listen to me; I will teach you the fear of the Lord. Which of you desires life, and covets many days to enjoy good? Keep your tongue from evil, and your lips from speaking deceit. Depart from evil, and do good; seek peace, and pursue it. The eyes of the Lord are on the righteous, and his ears are open to their cry. The face of the Lord is against evildoers, to cut off the remembrance of them from the earth.

Psalm 34:11-16

TIPS ON THE TOPIC

- Talking about Bonhoeffer may lead to discussions of the Holocaust. You will need to decide whether or not to approach this subject and how to deal with it. Do the youth know what the Holocaust is?
- Some youth have personally experienced evil. Be prepared for their stories to touch on difficult issues, such as child abuse and addictions.
- **Discussion Starter:** Have you ever taken a stand against some form of evil in your life? Describe the experience.

He was hanged for treason in April 1945, just months before Germany fell to the Allies.

Personal Views

Dietrich Bonhoeffer's witness is incredibly powerful. He showed that Christian discipleship calls for a costly involvement in the world's suffering. In fact, he believed Christians are identified not by how religious they are, but by how they participate in the suffering of God in the life of the world. Bonhoeffer himself felt called to suffer with the Jews, to stand with them against the evil that was Nazism. Who are you called to stand up for, no matter the cost?

Bonhoeffer believed that we are asked to embrace the world, its people and their pain, following the example of Jesus. Christ exists today as the Church, but Bonhoeffer was quick to say that the Church is much more than a building or tradition. The Church is the body of Christ, and in this mystery, all persons are united as one people in God. Working together as agents of God's reconciling love, the Church is called to stand in solidarity with non-Christians to confront evil and the powers of darkness. Does the Church accept Bonhoeffer's challenge today? Do we need to change our view of the Church to meet that challenge?

Bonhoeffer defined faith as discipleship, following Christ into the dark places of the world. This is a difficult road to walk. But the power of God is a present reality in the world, made manifest in an individual's or group's costly discipleship. As Bonhoeffer faced Nazism, we are led by God's grace to face the darkness and live so that God's light will shine there. Is there a dark place where you can bring God's light?

Almighty God, who created us in your own image: Grant us grace fearlessly to contend against evil and to make no peace with oppression; and, that we may reverently use our freedom, help us to employ it in the maintenance of justice in our communities and among the nations, to the glory of your holy Name; through Jesus Christ our Lord, who lives and reigns with you and the Holy Spirit, one God, now and for ever. *Amen.*

For Social Justice
The Book of Common Prayer, p. 260

Coming Together

(Time est: 10-15 min)

Display Resource Poster No. 5 called *Hear See Speak.* Tape a large piece of butcher paper or newsprint to the wall beneath the poster, or spread a long sheet on the floor. Place markers, pens, and crayons nearby. As the youth enter, ask them to draw a picture or image of evil. If young people are working individually, ask them to post their drawings around the room as they finish.

After everyone has gathered, ask the youth to find *Psalm 34:11-16* in their Bibles. Select a lector to lead the following prayer (Session Leaflet, p. 2).

Lector: *Let us pray.*
Dear God, we pray that in our lives we might find our purpose and carry it out, even in the face of evil. We pray we can do this even if we have to die, as Dietrich Bonhoeffer did. Amen.

Sarah, Grade 7

Lector: *A reading from Psalms, chapter 34, verses 11 through 16.*
(Full text on p. 2)
Lector: *The Word of the Lord.*
People: *Thanks be to God.*

Engaging

(Time est: 15-20 min)

Explain to the youth that we rarely look at evil squarely in the face. Today, however, with the pictures and images they have drawn, you are doing exactly that.

- How do those images make you feel? Are some more evil than others?
- What adjectives would you use to describe the pictures around the room?
- What do the images in the room have to do with you?
- What does the Resource Poster mean to you?

Tell the story of Dietrich Bonhoeffer. Be sure to mention the costly choices he made and his belief that a Christian is asked to embrace the world's suffering.

After you tell the story, engage the youth in a conversation about ways they face evil and the power of darkness in their lives.
- Do you see evil in your life or in the world today?
- What are the risks involved in facing evil?

Optional Activities

The following activities offer groups a wide range of choices. Consider the interests and strengths of youth and leaders and select those activity options that seem best suited to local time and talents. Remember no one can do everything!

Expressions
- **Diary:** Anne Frank was a Jewish teenager who for several years hid from the Nazis in an attic with her family. We know about Anne Frank because of a diary she kept during this anxious period. Imagine yourself hiding under similar circumstances. Write a diary entry for one day. Share the youth's "diaries," and read one or two entries from the actual *Diary of Anne Frank*.
- **Role play:** Ask the youth to place themselves at the scene when Bonhoeffer decides to return from the safety of the United States to Germany. Assign one person to be Bonhoeffer and others to be his friends and colleagues who want him to remain in the U.S.

Games
- **Ins and outs:** Arbitrarily assign youth to two groups and distinguish them in some physical way using two colors of crepe paper arm bands, or pin different patterns of material to their clothes. Treat the two groups in radically different ways: one group serves the snack, but is not allowed to have a snack themselves; the same group straightens the room while the other group watches; the first group must ask for permission to speak from someone in the other group. Because this can be a powerful experience, end it after a few minutes. Reverse the roles. Talk about the experience afterwards. What is the evil in each of us?

Media
Today's youth live in a media-rich culture that the Church cannot ignore. However, congregational norms about appropriate experiences vary and need to be respected. When choosing media activities consider local sentiments and prevailing laws covering public performances of copyrighted material.
- **Video:** Watch all or part of *Schindler's List* and discuss Schindler's courage. Why did he protect a group of Jews? (This movie is rated R and includes scenes that may not be appropriate for your group.) Or watch the older version of *Lord of the Flies* to see how a group of boys falls prey to their worst instincts. What does this movie have to say about the evil within each of us?
- **Print:** Design the front page of a newspaper that tells about the death of Bonhoeffer. Assign stories and pictures to be drawn by "sketch artists." Include a story about the progress of World War II at the time of his death.

Music
Music is important for today's youth and can be an integral part of youth experience in the context of Bible and Church activities. The music suggestions offered here reflect a broad variety of possibilities from simple listening to hearty music making. Seek out musicians within youth, church, and community groups to sing and play along.
- Read or sing together "Wilt thou forgive that sin, where I begun" (*The Hymnal 1982*, 141).
- Sing "God Will Take Care of You" (*Lift Every Voice and Sing*, 183).
- For a contemporary look at human sin and evil, listen to "Just the Way It Is," by Bruce Hornsby and the Range.

Service
- **Evil among us:** Discuss the existence of evil in your own community. How could this group do something about it? Youth might contact a shelter for women and children

WEAVINGS

- Schedule this session during a penitential season that would lend itself to a ritual for recognizing and letting go of sin.
- Despite his untimely death, Dietrich Bonhoeffer left us a legacy of his faith and courage through his *Letters and Papers from Prison*. He wrote about the importance of community in sustaining faith in books such as *Life Together*. Books based on his sermons and lectures also are widely available. Take time to discover Bonhoeffer for yourself.
- Sometimes we overlook the people who stand up to evil in spite of persecution and death. During World War II, the German Confessing Church confronted authorities and defied wrongful laws to speak out against terrible atrocities. Some people in other nations conquered by Germany also refused to obey edicts they knew to be evil. Today, people throughout the world defy evil by taking God's light into the darkness. Pray for the lights that shine even in the midst of terrible darkness.

RESOURCE POSTER

- Hear See Speak (No. 5)

who are the victims of domestic violence and discover the needs there. They could gather toys for the children, collect clothes, or buy cleaning supplies.
- **Prisoners:** Contact Amnesty International for information about prisoners of conscience in the world today. Write or call the organization about ways the group could help. Address: 322 8th Avenue; New York, NY 10001. Telephone: 212-807-8400 (East coast), 213-388-1327 (West coast).

Sharing
- **Worship:** Plan a service of healing and reconciliation using *The Book of Common Prayer*, p. 447, for the entire parish. Discovering the things done and left undone is only part of the task. Create a ritual that helps everyone face sin and then let go of it. Participants could write out their sins on slips of paper that are gathered and burned. The youth could also build a cross on which each person nails his or her sins.

Study
- **Holocaust:** Find out more about Nazi Germany and the Holocaust. Visit the library or contact a local organization that keeps Holocaust memories alive.
- **Racism:** Bonhoeffer was moved by the blight of racism in the United States when he was a student in the thirties. Read books about race in the U.S., such as *Black Like Me*, a story of racism written in the 1960's, or the more contemporary *Black Ice* by Lorene Cary, an autobiographical story about one of the first black students at an Episcopal school in New Hampshire.

Voices
Read and discuss the following quotations (Session Leaflet, p. 2).

Christ kept himself from suffering till his hour had come, but when it did come he met it as a free man, seized it, and mastered it...We are not Christ, but if we want to be Christians, we must have some share in Christ's large heartedness by acting with responsibility and in freedom when the hour of danger comes...

Jesus Christ lived in the midst of his enemies. At the end all of his disciples deserted him. On the cross he was utterly alone, surrounded by evildoers and mockers...So the Christian, too, belongs not in the seclusion of a cloistered life but in the thick of foes.
Dietrich Bonhoeffer

Fear of something is the root of hate for others, and hate within will eventually destroy the hater.
George Washington Carver

All that is necessary for the triumph of evil is that good [people] do nothing.
Edmund Burke

NOTES

Going Forth
Gather the group for a closing prayer and dismissal. Read together the prayer on page 823 of *The Book of Common Prayer* (also on p. 3 of the Session Leaflet).

Leader: *Let us pray.*
Grant, O God, that your holy and life-giving Spirit may so move every human heart, that barriers which divide us may crumble, suspicions disappear, and hatreds cease; that our divisions being healed, we may live in justice and peace; through Jesus Christ our Lord. Amen.
For Social Justice
The Book of Common Prayer, p. 823

Leader: *Let us go forth into the world, rejoicing in the power of the Spirit.*
People: *Thanks be to God.*

Look For
Are youth able to discuss the role of Christians in facing evil? Can they list ways that God helps them confront evil? Do they understand the importance of the community of the Church in resisting evil?

Oscar Romero: Taking a Stand
Called through Faith

Objective
This session focuses on the courage of Oscar Romero in the face of oppression. Youth will be able to discuss ways the Church can speak out for the poor and powerless. They will name ways they can stand up for others at their school or in their community who are rejected by the mainstream.

Background for Leaders
The Commentary for this session describes the life of Oscar Romero after he was named archbishop of El Salvador. A key name is Romero; key places are San Salvador and the Metropolitan Cathedral; the key event is the assassination of Romero. For spiritual preparation think about economic justice for all people.

Commentary
Oscar Arnulfo Romero was born in 1917 in Ciudad Barrios, El Salvador and ordained a Roman Catholic priest in 1942. He was a moderate, well-liked cleric, who had little interest in politics. When he was elected Archbishop of San Salvador, the highest ranking official of the Roman Catholic Church in El Salvador, most people believed he would offer no trouble to El Salvador's wealthy ruling class.

But in 1977, the year of his election, political tensions were mounting. Historically, El Salvador is a country where the vast majority of the wealth and property is held by only a dozen or so families, while the rest of the people are caught in desperate poverty. The ruling families were content with their non-threatening, religious leaders and with keeping the status quo in the country, preserved with repression and violence.

A few weeks after the new archbishop was consecrated, gunmen murdered two parishioners and their priest, Rutilio Grande, an admired pastor in one of El Salvador's small towns. Romero said these murders were like a call from God, awaking him to the extreme suffering of his people. All over the country, authorities arrested and brutally beat peasants who often disappeared, never to be seen again. They also ransacked churches and left them in ruins. The archbishop began preaching against the violence in his weekly sermons at the Metropolitan Cathedral in San Salvador, where hundreds gathered to listen to his gospel of liberation. Hundreds of thousands more heard his message on the radio.

Four more times Romero buried priests killed by forces allied with the government, never shrinking from condemning their actions. Moreover, he condemned the violence perpetrated by guerrillas representing the peasants.

Death threats became commonplace for Romero, but he never stopped calling for a re-distribution of his country's wealth and an end to violence. On Monday, March 24,

SESSION LEAFLET

■ **Art**—*Oscar Romero*, by Bobbi Tull

■ **Key Verse**—*For to me, living is Christ and dying is gain.*
—Philippians 1:21

■ **Youth Commentary and Prayer**

■ **Voices**—Jorge Lara-Braud, Chester Himes, Elizabeth Rundle Charles

■ **Daily Reflections**

■ **Words to Remember**

■ **Prayer**—For the Oppressed (BCP, p. 826)

LECTOR'S TEXT

Yes, and I will continue to rejoice, for I know that through your prayers and the help of the Spirit of Jesus Christ this will turn out for my deliverance. It is my eager expectation and hope that I will not be put to shame in any way, but that by my speaking with all boldness, Christ will be exalted now as always in my body, whether by life or by death. For to me, living is Christ and dying is gain. If I am to live in the flesh, that means fruitful labor for me; and I do not know which I prefer. I am hard pressed between the two: my desire is to depart and be with Christ, for that is far better; but to remain in the flesh is more necessary for you.

Philippians 1:18b-24

TIPS ON THE TOPIC

- Youth may want to know if El Salvador has changed since Romero's death. Bring in a current article about El Salvador to share with the group.
- Be prepared to answer questions about the United States' involvement in the violence in El Salvador. However, don't get sidetracked from the central point of one man's stance against oppression.
- **Discussion Starter:** Have you ever been affected by some else's courage? How did it change you?

1980, Romero was shot once in the heart by a sharpshooter's bullet as he celebrated Mass. While his voice was silenced, his message lived on.

Personal Views

"In the name of God, in the name of this suffering people whose laments rise to the heavens each day...I beg you, I beseech you, I order you, to stop the repression," cried Archbishop Oscar Romero in his last Sunday sermon before his death. In the week before his assassination, 150 people died in political violence in El Salvador, and 25 more died on the day he spoke these words. Romero used his position to protest on behalf of the poor, and his death became a symbol for those who sought peace and change in his country.

Romero was an unlikely prophet. His election as archbishop came precisely because of his lack of political activity. But he was transformed by the death of a fellow priest, a brother. By extension, the people of El Salvador who were suffering under a cruel regime were his brothers and sisters, as well. He began to use his voice to speak for the voiceless.

Societies have a way of pushing some people to the margin, where they suffer neglect or abuse. Poor people don't choose to be poor; they are often trapped there by circumstances beyond their control. Christians are called not to judge poor people, but to judge poverty itself, and to work for economic justice for everyone. Mary in the *Gospel of Luke*, and Hannah before her in *I Samuel*, sing a song of God's care for the poor. "He raises up the poor from the dust; he lifts the needy from the ash heap, to make them sit with princes and inherit a seat of honor." (*I Samuel 2:8a*)

O God, who created all peoples in your image, we thank you for the wonderful diversity of races and cultures in this world. Enrich our lives by ever-widening circles of fellowship, and show us your presence in those who differ most from us, until our knowledge of your love is made perfect in our love for all your children; through Jesus Christ our Lord. Amen.

For the Diversity of Races and Cultures
The Book of Common Prayer, p. 840

Coming Together

(Time est: 10-15 min)

Play some quiet music in the background as the youth begin to come into the room. Ask the youth to create a "sanctuary" for themselves that is a comfortable, safe place. Encourage them to move furniture, spread out on the floor, and even turn out the lights. After everyone has found a place, ask the group to sit in silence for a few moments.

After the brief silence, when everyone has gathered, ask the youth to find *Philippians 1:18b-24* in their Bibles. Select a lector to lead the following prayer (Session Leaflet, p. 2).

Lector: *Let us pray.*
Dear God, please make the violence stop. I know it is a hard thing to do, but help us try to stop the violence. I know that you want all of your people to be safe. Amen.
Lauren, Grade 7

Lector: *A reading from Paul's Letter to the Philippians, chapter 1, verses 18b through 24.*
(Full text on p. 2)
Lector: *The Word of the Lord.*
People: *Thanks be to God.*

Engaging

(Time est: 15-20 min)

Ask the youth to describe how they chose their place in the room and if they felt more comfortable being in a place they had created for themselves.

- What made this place a sanctuary for you?
- How do we create places where people can truly be themselves?
- Where is the sanctuary in our church?
- Do you think the church itself is a sanctuary? Is it a place where people can be themselves or be safe? Why or why not?
- Do you feel safe exploring your faith at this church?

Display Resource Poster No. 6 of a church in Central America. Tell the story of Oscar Romero. Be sure to relate that the Church in El Salvador for many years was not a place where people could safely voice their opinions about their country's oppressive government. Romero opened the doors of his parish to people who

were in danger because of their political opinions. His death raised consciousness about repression, and it shamed the perpetrators of violence.
- Where are places of violence and poverty that are closer to home?
- What can you do about violence and poverty in your community or city?

Optional Activities

The following activities offer groups a wide range of choices. Consider the interests and strengths of youth and leaders and select those activity options that seem best suited to local time and talents. Remember no one can do everything!

Expressions
- **Prayer book:** Create a collection of prayers for safety and protection. Read the prayers "For Social Justice" (BCP, p. 823) and "In Times of Conflict" (BCP, p. 824). Look at the service of Compline (BCP, p. 127), especially at pages 132-135. Include prayers from *The Book of Common Prayer* that you find helpful. Using these prayers as a guide, compose prayers to add to the collection. Suggest the youth keep the prayer books in their rooms or near their beds.
- **Crosses:** In El Salvador the people decorate crosses with brightly painted images from their everyday lives: their crops, livestock, school teachers, chalk boards, helicopters, pictures of themselves, and heroes who have lost their lives fighting for justice. Draw or make crosses and decorate them with symbols of justice, sanctuary, and people you love.

Games
- **Sardines:** The object of the Sardine game is to find the person who is "Romero." The youth are now the "Peasants." "Romero" hides while the Peasants look for him or her, seeking safety. All Peasants are welcomed into "Romero's" hiding place—there's always room for one more! The game is over when all the Peasants are all safe.

Media
Today's youth live in a media-rich culture that the Church cannot ignore. However, congregational norms about appropriate experiences vary and need to be respected. When choosing media activities consider local sentiments and prevailing laws covering public performances of copyrighted material.
- **Video:** Raul Julia stars in *Romero*, an excellent portrayal of Oscar Romero's life and witness. Watch it for background material or show it to youth at a longer session.
- **Print:** Bring in newspapers and news magazines and ask the youth to find current articles about injustice or racism. Look for places that are not safe, where people may be looking for sanctuary.

Music
Music is important for today's youth and can be an integral part of youth experience in the context of Bible and Church activities. The music suggestions offered here reflect a broad variety of possibilities from simple listening to hearty music making. Seek out musicians within youth, church, and community groups to sing and play along.
- Read or sing together "Where cross the crowded ways of life," (*The Hymnal 1982*, 609) that touches on the theme of justice.
- Sing "Do Not Fear to Hope" (*Gather*, GIA Publications, Inc., 420). In the second verse, what are we to do "when victory seems out of justice's sight"?
- There are a number of contemporary songs that have expressions of safety. Ask the youth to share the lyrics of one they know.

Service
- **Companions:** Find out if your parish or diocese has a companion relationship with a parish in a developing country. Companion dioceses share resources and pray for each other. Write letters to teenagers in a companion church to discover what their lives are like today. Encourage the youth to create their own relationships with young people in a country where safety and poverty are serious concerns.

WEAVINGS

- This session could be scheduled near March 24, the date of Oscar Romero's assassination.
- "Sanctuary" is defined as a sacred or holy place, like a church or temple. The word also means a place that provides refuge or where fugitives are immune from arrest. Romero used his parish church as a sanctuary, providing a safe place for people in political danger.
- To protest the unfair distribution of land and wealth in El Salvador, the peasants destroyed tons of coffee beans. For years the peasants worked to plant and harvest the beans, but never benefitted from the enormous wealth produced by their labor. Their action of protest is similar to the Boston Tea Party when patriots in America protested being taxed without fair representation. When is a rebellion against authority justified? What is our responsibility to speak for those who have no power?

RESOURCE POSTER

- Worshipping Together (No. 6)

Sharing

- **Decorate:** Hang the crosses made for the Expressions activity somewhere in your church or "sanctuary." The youth could select one or two of the designs to decorate the cover of the prayer books they compiled.

Study

- **On the net:** Unfortunately, not much information has been published about Oscar Romero. If you have access to the Internet, search for Oscar Romero to learn more about his life and ministry.
- **Migrant labor:** Learn about the plight of migrant farm workers in the United States. Compare their situation with the agrarian reform in El Salvador.
- **Update:** Find out how the political situation has changed since Romero's death in 1980. Have the disparities between rich and poor diminished?

Voices

Read and discuss the following quotations (Session Leaflet, p. 2).

Together with thousands of Salvadorans, I have seen Jesus. This time his name was Oscar Arnulfo Romero. His broken body is broken with the body of Jesus, his shed blood is shed with the blood of Jesus. And as with Jesus, so it is with Monsignor, he died for us that we might live in freedom and in love and justice for one another. His resurrection is not a future event. It is a present reality.
— Jorge Lara-Braud
At Romero's funeral

Martyrs are needed to create incidents. Incidents are needed to create revolutions. Revolutions are needed to create progress.
— Chester Himes

To know how to say what other people only think, is what makes [people] poets and sages; and to dare to say what others only dare to think, makes [people] martyrs or reformers.
— Elizabeth Rundle Charles

NOTES

Going Forth

Gather the group for a closing prayer and dismissal. Read together the prayer on page 826 of *The Book of Common Prayer* (also on p. 3 of the Session Leaflet).

Leader: *Let us pray.*
Look with pity, O heavenly Father, upon the people in this land who live with injustice, terror, disease, and death as their constant companions. Have mercy upon us. Help us to eliminate our cruelty to these our neighbors. Strengthen those who spend their lives establishing equal protection of the law and equal opportunities for all. And grant that every one of us may enjoy a fair portion of the riches of this land; through Jesus Christ our Lord. Amen.
For the Oppressed
The Book of Common Prayer, p. 826

Leader: *Let us go forth into the world, rejoicing in the power of the Spirit.*
People: *Thanks be to God.*

Look For

Are youth about to discuss how the Church speaks out for the poor and powerless? Are they able to identify those who are rejected by the mainstream? Can the youth name ways they can stand up for others at their schools or in their community?